More Praise for *The Safe Child Handbook*

"This handbook has wonderfully addressed the question, How can parents acknowledge real contemporary fears and help assure their children's safety, and at the same time promote their children's independence?"
—*Timothy F. Dugan, M.D., senior consultant in education,
Cambridge Hospital, Division of Child and Adult Psychiatry*

"This guide offers many useful ideas about keeping children safe, but its chief contributions are the two chapters on how you and your children can cope with fear most effectively. The activities described there will prove invaluable in maintaining your family's mental health in these troubling times. These are helpful methods for reducing anxiety in parents and children."
—*Gordon L. Ulrey, Ph.D., associate clinical professor of psychology,
School of Medicine, University of California at Davis*

"As a pediatrician, I have dealt with the fears and phobias of children. When these are compounded by parental anxieties, the challenges of addressing the problems are magnified. The world is full of potential dangers, many of which are captured by the media who bring distant problems into our homes. *The Safe Child Handbook* offers a practical and insightful approach and is a valuable guide to both parents and professionals."
—*Carol Berkowitz, M.D., executive vice chair and professor,
Department of Pediatrics, Harbor-UCLA Medical Center,
David Geffen School of Medicine at UCLA*

"As a parent, teacher, and community activist, I am acutely aware of the dangers that are both unavoidable and, at times, out of our control. This book provides accurate information and simple strategies to encourage people to be proactive, and promotes communication between those who care for children and the children who put their trust in us."
—*Joan Davidson, M.A., past president, Palos Verdes Peninsula Unified
School District; art educator, Torrance Unified School District*

THE SAFE CHILD HANDBOOK

THE SAFE CHILD HANDBOOK

How to Protect Your Family and Cope with Anxiety in a Threat-Filled World

John S. Dacey, Ph.D.
Lisa B. Fiore, Ph.D.

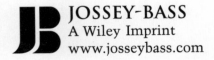

JOSSEY-BASS
A Wiley Imprint
www.josseybass.com

Published by Jossey-Bass
A Wiley Imprint
989 Market Street, San Francisco, CA 94103-1741   www.josseybass.com

Jossey-Bass books and products are available through most bookstores. To contact Jossey-Bass directly call our Customer Care Department within the U.S. at 800-956-7739, outside the U.S. at 317-572-3986, or fax 317-572-4002.

Jossey-Bass also publishes its books in a variety of electronic formats. Some content that appears in print may not be available in electronic books.

Library of Congress Cataloging-in-Publication Data

Dacey, John S.
    The safe child handbook : how to protect your family and cope with anxiety in a threat-filled world / John S. Dacey, and Lisa B. Fiore.
        p. cm.
    Includes bibliographical references and index.
    ISBN-13: 978-0-7879-8688-9 (pbk.)
    ISBN-10: 0-7879-8688-7 (pbk.)
    1. Safety education—United States.   2. Child rearing—United States.   3. Children's accidents—United States—Prevention.   4. Children—United States—Conduct of life.
I. Fiore, Lisa B., date-   II. Title.
    HQ770.7.D33   2006
    649'.10289—dc22   2006014174

Printed in the United States of America
FIRST EDITION
PB Printing   10 9 8 7 6 5 4 3 2 1

This book is lovingly dedicated to:

My nine grandchildren—Brianna, Liam, Madelyn, Nicholas, Benjamin, Téa, James, Quinn, and Lucas—whose safety and serenity mean the world to me.—J.S.D.

Matthew, the "can-do kid," and Tinker-Talia, who inspire me every day with their wisdom, humor, and innocence.—L.B.F.

CONTENTS

ACKNOWLEDGMENTS

In the preparation of a book such as this, scouring the literature for the best research findings and advice to parents could not be accomplished adequately by one or even two authors. We had a lot of help from a team of dedicated students at Boston College and from our friends over the five years it took to complete the work. We acknowledge gratefully the contribution of the following: Abby Kritzler, Alice Dunne, Annie Leese, Arar Han, Barbara Crane, Bridget Shanley, Caitlin Graboski, Chris Calcagni, Christine Murphy, Courtney White, Denise Wallingford, Eddie Castro, Elizabeth Auty, Emily Kearns, Erica Lolli, Erin Kelly, Janet Lane, Janet Smith, Jenn Wadenius, Jess Tansey, Jonathon Evans, Judy Robinson, Kim Dziama, Kristen Gearin, Laura Hayden, Lauren Bernstein, Lauren Gilfeather, Lauren Szewczyk, Liz McClure, Liz Rini, Lowell Schulman, Lizzie Nyitray, Martha Wirecki, Megan Bushey, Meghan McBride, Melanie Kay, Monica Carty, Rich Sanzo, Shelley-Anne Quilty, Stacy Phelan, Timothy Dugan, and Tim Brown.

And then there are those individuals whose unselfish donation of their time calls for them to be mentioned separately. The following individuals shared their opinions and editing skills for all or part of the book: Jennifer Allen, Juliette Fay, Kristen Iwai, Elyse Pratt, Robin Tartaglia, and Diane Wallace.

We are deeply grateful for the advice and encouragement of our agent at the Gail Ross Agency, Howard Yoon, and our editor at

Jossey-Bass, Seth Schwartz. Without the creativity of these two gentlemen, our work would be much the poorer. We also thank the staff at Jossey-Bass—Alan Rinzler, Jennifer Wenzel, and Carol Hartland—for their assistance.

Finally, the two people who contributed the most were our spouses, Linda Dacey and Stephen Fiore. We can't thank you enough!

THE SAFE
CHILD
HANDBOOK

Loving Spirit, give us grace to accept with serenity the things
    that cannot be changed,
The courage to change the things which should be changed, and
The wisdom to know the difference.

—*Reinhold Niebuhr*

1

"DOING TOO MUCH IS AS RISKY AS DOING TOO LITTLE"

Theologian Reinhold Niebuhr's much-cited serenity prayer on the opposite page precisely frames the modern parent's dilemma: no matter how hard you try, you can't eliminate risk. You can't know *all* the actions you could take that might make your family a little safer, and even if you could, you'd never find the time to accomplish such a herculean task. In fact, you would only increase the anxiety levels of your children, your spouse, and yourself. As our research makes clear, the solution lies in having the wisdom to know where the line between action and acceptance lies. This book is about finding that line.

The task is not simple, as Margaret Delano knows well:

MOTHERING IS NO PIECE OF CAKE

An intelligent and creative person, Margaret is known for her sympathetic nature. If you're having a problem, she's the one you look to. Margaret runs a small mail order business from her home that she started eleven years ago. She designs, produces, and markets greeting cards. She was not an easy-going woman in the past, but since the kidnapping of Elizabeth Smart, she sees the world as a much more threatening place.

She and her husband, Dave, have three children. Helen is sixteen, Jimmy is ten, and Colette is five. Margaret worries about each of them. When she takes Colette to the park, she seldom talks to the other women there. She is nervous that she'll be distracted for a moment and someone will snatch her daughter. Although she realizes this is unlikely, she doesn't want to take any chances.

Margaret used to let Jimmy play baseball in the afternoon with his friends, but then she learned that a man was arrested for trying to sell marijuana at Jimmy's middle school. She now insists that Jimmy come straight home at the end of school, which causes frequent arguments between them. Although her daughter Helen considers herself to be independent, Margaret tries to protect her with regular warnings. She suspects that behind her back, Helen usually disregards her cautions. She is right. Helen thinks her mother is an excessive worrier who is more overprotective than her friends' mothers.

Whenever one of the kids has a class trip or excursion, Margaret often takes time off from work to be one of the chaperones. She lets her parents or her in-laws drive the kids only when absolutely necessary. She thinks that at their age, they are unlikely to be safe drivers.

Dave, Margaret's husband, occasionally gets irritated by what he views as Margaret's excessive concern. He knows life presents certain dangers, but he thinks her belief that catastrophe is just around the corner makes matters worse. "There's really not much we can do. Can't you just relax?" has become his mantra. Although he loves Margaret deeply and wants to be supportive, Dave often feels frustrated by his inability to make suggestions she can accept.

Margaret wants to be more relaxed about life. She knows there is a high price to pay for her constant vigilance. She feels resentful that the job of protecting loved ones and watching for trouble rests squarely on her shoulders. Yet she also knows that her apprehension is excessive. She is aware that her attitude is driving a wedge between Helen and her. And perhaps worst of all, the two younger kids are developing into worrywarts. Jimmy's sleep is increasingly fitful, and she can't help noticing that Colette is reluctant to try anything new.

"I know I can't protect them from every possible danger," she thinks, "but I can't just turn a blind eye to the risks out there either. I just wish I knew if we're doing enough—or maybe too much!"

A MOTHER'S EIGHT MAIN CONCERNS

First, let us say that we would prefer to address this book to male and female parents, but as most research makes clear, it is mothers who take on primary responsibility for the safety of their children. Some fathers contribute significantly, but moms, for good or ill, are much more likely to shoulder this particular responsibility. You mothers are the ones telling pollsters that you are more worried now than ever before. It's no wonder that you are because, objectively, the world has become more dangerous. One might think if you're not a worried mom, you haven't been paying attention. A careful perusal of recent Census Bureau statistics indicates that although some things have improved in our world, there really are more dangers out there, as you can see in Figure 1.1.

When our book, *Your Anxious Child,* was published in 2000, no one could have anticipated the flood of alarming news and tragic events that occurred in subsequent years. Yet in a post-9/11, around-the-clock news culture, we are bombarded with images and messages about threats to our families—everything from mad cow disease and avian flu to kids suffocating in the trunks of cars and teens being abducted in the tropics. There is the ever-present danger of global terrorism and the impending likelihood of another domestic terrorist attack. Even the weather appears to be going haywire. It comes as no surprise that the surgeon general recently reported that 13 percent of children in this country have a diagnosable anxiety order—a 30 percent increase from ten years ago.

A recent Roper poll confirms these trends. According to Roper, parents voiced eight primary concerns related to the well-being of

FIGURE 1.1. The Good News/Bad News Scale

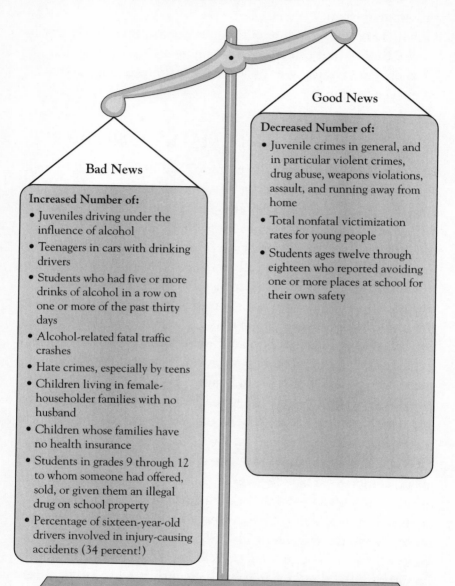

Good News

Decreased Number of:

- Juvenile crimes in general, and in particular violent crimes, drug abuse, weapons violations, assault, and running away from home
- Total nonfatal victimization rates for young people
- Students ages twelve through eighteen who reported avoiding one or more places at school for their own safety

Bad News

Increased Number of:

- Juveniles driving under the influence of alcohol
- Teenagers in cars with drinking drivers
- Students who had five or more drinks of alcohol in a row on one or more of the past thirty days
- Alcohol-related fatal traffic crashes
- Hate crimes, especially by teens
- Children living in female-householder families with no husband
- Children whose families have no health insurance
- Students in grades 9 through 12 to whom someone had offered, sold, or given them an illegal drug on school property
- Percentage of sixteen-year-old drivers involved in injury-causing accidents (34 percent!)

their families: weather emergencies, kidnapping, terrorism, inappropriate media influences, drugs and alcohol, child abuse, school violence, and home safety. Furthermore, we now know that the more diligent a parent is about defending the family from these dangers, the more likely she or he is to suffer from a serious anxiety reaction. Sadly, it seems that the harder parents try to keep their children safe, the greater the chance is that they will pass their fears on to their children. Life is a question of balancing costs and benefits, and nowhere is this truer than in facing the newest challenges to our equanimity.

For the past four years, we have led teams of our students at Boston College and Lesley University to help us investigate the nature of these threats and survey the multitudinous lists of possible solutions for dealing with each of them. Forty students, mostly at the graduate level, have assisted us in conducting research on this topic. We have examined studies of precisely how dangerous these perils are, in what ways they threaten families, and recommendations for diminishing the risks they represent. We have sifted through the newest literature on how anxiety can best be reduced in the face of real perils. Finally, we have interviewed dozens of parents (mostly mothers) to get their reaction to this information and to have them share dramatic stories about how they overcame—or felt overwhelmed by—the threats they perceived or experienced in their lives.

Through our search of the literature, we have discovered that in addition to these eight threats to the family, there are a number of other crosscurrents that cause stress for mothers. When you understand these changes, you can see why many of you feel more threatened than your mothers and grandmothers did. These are the major shifts:

- *Role overload.* Being a woman in a Western culture, you are increasingly affected by an overload of responsibilities. Because many of you raise a family and are employed full time, there is a distinct onus on mothers to do both. Most women today work outside the home more than their mothers did. Studies indicate that the average mother with a full-time job outside the home also does between 65 and 85 percent of the housework. There are only so many hours in the day, but if you are a typical mother, you are also expected to spend a lot of time with each of your children. If you can't, you feel guilty. You may also feel that you have to compensate for your busy husband, who often works extra hours too. Men typically work fifty-one hours per week in this country and women forty-one, the longest workweeks in the world. The average father spends less than thirty minutes a day of one-on-one interaction with his children, about one-third as much as the mother. This pressure is reflected in the number of mothers who work full time. For those with a child under age one, the percentage declined from 59 percent in 1997 to 53 percent in 2002, and for those with a child under age three, the percentages for those two years dropped from 61 to 58.

• *Perfection overload.* There is also the common belief that whatever our children do, they must do it as perfectly as possible: the best grades, the most activities, and so on. Otherwise, it is said, they will be disadvantaged and will fall behind in a race for the top that is all too real. This is a problem for mothers also. As Judith Warner documents in her new book, *Perfect Madness: Motherhood in the Age of Anxiety* (2006), an essential part of this myth is that it demands the suppression of a mother's personal ambitions. If you want some success yourself at anything other than being a perfect mother, goes the myth, you ought to feel ashamed of your selfishness.

• *The hurried family.* Psychologist David Elkind's best-selling book, *The Hurried Child* (2001), received a lot of attention when it was first published in 1981. In this book, he argued that modern parents try to force their children to be "superkids," excessively bent on perfection in every area of their lives. Today we need to be concerned for the hurried *family.* After-school hours and weekends are now filled with so many organized activities there is virtually no time for unplanned and unstructured moments to spend together. No time is wasted. Children in such families need adults to arrange and conduct their interactions (hence the so-called soccer mom).

They are more dependent on their mothers than kids were in previous generations, another factor making your role as mother more stressful.

- *"Scientific parenting."* There has been a plethora of scientific articles and books in recent years on the nature of human development. Most of this research has been on the brain, but other aspects have been studied as well. Even worse, many authors try to persuade us that their *recommendations* for parenting are scientific and irrefutable. (If only every child came with his or her own personal instruction manual.) Nevertheless, mothers who have been reading these books frequently believe that there is one right way to parent, if only they could figure it out!

- *Increasing age of mother at birth of child.* Average maternal age at childbirth has been increasing. If you are in your thirties, forties, or fifties, you probably have less energy and endurance than you did in your twenties, two assets that are essential to this vocation of motherhood. Older mothers often speak of the strain of keeping up with their active kids all day.

- *Shrinking family size.* The size of the average American family has been steadily shrinking. When the family is smaller, mothers can attend to each child more easily. As a result, children have less independent time and are more likely to be dependent on their mothers in many ways. This "learned helplessness" may also make your role more difficult. True, you probably have fewer children than your grandmother did, but you are also likely to have significantly less help.

- *Lack of extended family help.* Extended family members (grandparents, aunts and uncles, cousins) are no longer likely to live nearby. This means that you probably have less help than mothers in the past, which puts more pressure on you. It has been said, "Only six people can raise a child." In other words, the only people who are intrinsically vested enough in a child to get really excited about his or her accomplishments are the child's parents and grandparents. Also, the counsel of extended family members who know your children well may be more helpful than advice from others.

Together, these forces certainly put pressure on you. They may color your evaluation of how dangerous your environment is. Would you like to get insight into just how much the threats in your world are bothering you personally?

YOUR AQ (ANXIETY QUOTIENT)

To calculate your level of anxiety, decide which of four categories best describes how each of the following statements is like you: VLM = very like me, LM = like me, NLM = not like me, and VUM = very unlike me. (It doesn't have to be something you actually do; it just has to be something that sounds like your values.) When you have picked the category that best describes your attitude toward the statement, circle the number next to the question. For example, if statement 2 is like you, circle 2 on that line. When you are done, add up your total score.

Statements	VLM	LM	NLM	VUM
1. I believe my child should be seated in the safest place in the classroom.	4	3	2	1
2. I would let my ten-year-old son go on a scout campout in winter if I were confident the leader would pay attention to weather and other dangers.	1	2	3	4
3. It would be a good idea to get plans for making a chemical safe room in my house in case of a germ warfare attack.	4	3	2	1

Statements	VLM	LM	NLM	VUM
4. Before I open the door of my car at night, I look in the back seat with the flashlight that I carry with me.	4	3	2	1
5. I would buy a computer program that would let me monitor my fifteen-year-old daughter's incoming and outgoing e-mails.	4	3	2	1
6. I would allow my thirteen-year-old son to take the train into the city to go shopping if he's with a friend.	1	2	3	4
7. I believe that storing gallons and gallons of bottled water is really quite unnecessary.	1	2	3	4
8. I have no idea how the electrical system in our house works.	1	2	3	4
9. I would absolutely monitor my daughter's diary if I thought she might be doing something that would compromise her safety.	4	3	2	1
10. On rare occasions, I have ducked into a store while one of the kids was sitting in the car.	1	2	3	4

(Continued)

Statements	VLM	LM	NLM	VUM
11. I really feel that most movie moguls ought to be ashamed of themselves for profiting so much from featuring sex, violence, and stereotypes.	4	3	2	1
12. I am absolutely certain that I know what movies my children are seeing.	4	3	2	1
13. I think it just makes sense to avoid people who have a foreign appearance.	4	3	2	1
14. I have no fear of attending events that are crowded.	1	2	3	4
15. I would be happy if my children never took a single drink their whole lives.	4	3	2	1
16. I am against all the bans on alcohol advertising; they are anti-capitalistic and anti-American.	1	2	3	4
17. I have a lot of doubts about the ability of schools to keep our kids safe.	4	3	2	1
18. One of the greatest dangers our children face today is from drug dealers.	4	3	2	1
19. The violence in video games like Grand Theft Auto is no worse than what				

Statements	VLM	LM	NLM	VUM
kids see on television every night of the week.	1	2	3	4
20. Most teachers have no idea of how to deal with violent students.	4	3	2	1
21. You are more likely to get hit by lightning than you are to be injured in a terrorist attack.	1	2	3	4

TOTAL SCORE

The lowest possible score, 21, indicates that you are probably a rather relaxed, nonworrying person. The highest score, 84, indicates that you're quite anxious about the dangers in the world. If your score is above 42, we recommend that you seriously consider carrying out as many of the activities offered in Chapters Ten and Eleven as you and your family can.

You may also want to check on your level of anxiety for each of the threats to safety. You can compile that score by adding up your numbers by threat type. For home safety, look at numbers 3, 7, and 8; for terrorism, 13, 14, and 21; for school violence, 1, 17, and 20; for media influence, 11, 12, and 19; for drugs and alcohol, 15, 16, and 18; for child abuse, 2, 5, and 9; and for abduction, 4, 6, and 10.

WHAT YOU NEED TO DO

Whether your score on the AQ Test is moderate or astronomical, our recommendation is the same: if you and your family hope to confront the threats successfully (and if you as the mother want to handle the societal pressures we described), you must achieve three goals:

1. *You must make certain that your family has taken all reasonable precautions to protect yourselves in each of the eight areas.* This book will inform you about the existing level of threat in each case and will teach you precisely how to protect yourselves according to the advice of the best experts. However, many of the people we have interviewed and counseled have tried so hard to protect their children that they have actually made their situations more stressful (remember Margaret's story at the beginning of this chapter?). Therefore you also need to recognize that keeping your family safe can be a consuming task. You will need to know where to draw the line and where to strike a balance. Therefore, we will point out the kinds of actions that experts consider excessive as well.

2. *Over time, working to strengthen the family's safety will reduce each member's level of fear.* In the short run, however, it is likely to evoke strong emotions. Involving children in safety plans often makes them more fearful because they become more aware of the many dangers that exist. Safety planning will doubtless cause an even stronger fear reaction in children who already have a proclivity toward anxiety. Therefore, we have provided a series of techniques that are designed to help alleviate fear, in children and in teens, and we are tailoring the exercises for each step to apply to a threat area. These antianxiety exercises will help your kids avoid becoming overwhelmed by the family's preparations. You will find them in Chapter Ten. We urge you to dip into this chapter as you make your safety preparations. Don't wait to avail your family of these techniques until you have completed your safety arrangements. Your children are likely to benefit from them most if they are carried out from time to time as you do this work.

3. *Allay your own fears, and build family cohesion.* You and your partner are likely to experience some anxiety as a result of this work as well. Thus, we have devised a series of powerful activities you can use to do this. This third aspect of our approach is essential, since parents' fears almost always exacerbate those of their children. These adult activities are in Chapter Eleven. As with the child-

oriented activities, we urge you to refer to Chapter Eleven from time to time, especially if you or your partner experience anxious reactions to this work.

THE COPE PROGRAM

The anxiety-reduction methods for children in this book, and to some extent those for adults, follow the nationally tested COPE regimen. For the past twenty years, John Dacey has been experimenting with techniques for helping children and adolescents increase their self-control over their study habits and their ability to avoid using drugs. Lisa Fiore has joined him in this work for the past five years. During this time, the approach has been adapted specifically to alleviate anxiety problems. The letters in the acronym COPE stand for the four steps that make up the method:

C = Calming the nervous system

O = Originating an imaginative plan

P = Persisting in the face of obstacles and failure

E = Evaluating the plan

What we have discovered through our teaching, therapy work, and research studies is that most people, regardless of age, have similar problems when they deal with situations that are anxiety provoking. Most respond well to the four steps of COPE.

Calming the Nervous System

The first problem most of us confront when we enter a stressful situation is the stimulation of the fight-or-flight response. This is the ancient human tendency when under assault to either attack the antagonist or run away. In prehistoric times, this response was most functional; when Neanderthal humans were being eyed by a saber-toothed tiger as a possible lunch, standing around and thinking up alternative plans would have been fatal. Today, however, most situations that scare children cannot be resolved by simply running away or attacking. For example, as your child stands up in front of a class to make a presentation, she may feel like leaving, or she may feel angry with her classmates who are staring at her. What she needs to do is quell this neurological response to stress so that she can think clearly about what it is she wants to say and how she wants to say it. A calm nervous system, not a highly aroused one, is what she needs when dealing with most modern stressors.

In this book we cover different strategies for calming the nervous system. Some of them are physical, some mental, some a combination of the two, and some involve spiritual approaches. We provide numerous activities that your child may use to achieve tranquility.

Originating an Imaginative Plan

The second problem that anxious people often face is that even when calm, they often have faulty understandings of their feelings and why they have them. Furthermore, because they are under such pressure, they may be unable to think of really imaginative plans for dealing with their quandaries. Anxious children are less likely than others to have imaginative ideas about the best way to problem-solve, even though, with their vibrant imaginations, they often have greater creative potential. However, if they have calmed down their nervous systems, they can use the techniques that we teach to develop better insights into themselves and design an imaginative plan for dealing with their problem.

Research has identified a number of thinking strategies and styles that are much more likely to produce creative problem solving. We offer numerous activities that are aimed at helping you and your child to become better problem solvers. As you and she learn these techniques, you both will improve your ability to design a plan that will combat her anxiety.

Persisting in the Face of Obstacles and Failure

We have found that many plans for dealing with anxiety start out well, but then the person loses faith. The temptation to quit blossoms, and soon she gives up on her plan. A number of scholars have shown that people who believe in God or some other higher power or supernatural force are more likely to persevere when the going gets tough. Anxious children are especially prone to throwing in the towel. We offer a variety of paths that can be taken to help your child have faith in herself, her plan, and her "higher power." Among these paths is a new one about which we are very excited: techniques for designing your own family rituals that, when faithfully attended to, are proving to be powerful anxiety fighters.

Evaluating the Plan

Although having faith in your plan is important, whether it is really working is critical to your success. We recommend evaluation techniques be used both while the plan is in operation and after the plan has been carried out, so that improvements can be constructed. We suggest a number of ways you can get objective feedback on the efficacy of your plan.

As the mother of a modern family, you face a daunting task. You need to discern what actions to take to make your family safe, without overdoing it to the point that you and they become overwhelmed with fears and general anxiety. You need a unified strategy that is neither overly cautious nor irresponsibly inattentive. This applies not only to what you do but also to how you do it. A brilliant plan that your children cannot comprehend, or one that your partner doesn't like, may be worse than no plan at all. You need a strategy that makes sense within the context of your lives, one that makes each of you feel confident and leaves you and your family with an enthusiastic view of life. We sincerely hope and believe that with some adjustments for your family's personal preferences, the concepts and activities in this book will guide you all safely and soundly to that goal.

PART ONE

ENSURING YOUR CHILD'S SAFETY

2

WEATHER EMERGENCIES

"What's Going On with Mother Nature?"

We begin with a concern that wouldn't have been so high on the list in previous years. Greenhouse gases and the subsequent global warming are supposed to be the major cause, but whatever is behind it, there can be no doubt that the weather is disrupting lives and causing premature deaths all over the world. We believe that if you attend to the advice and checklists in this chapter, you and your family will be much less likely to be victimized by these alarming changes.

A RAILROAD RUNS THROUGH YOUR HOUSE

Fifth-grader Richie Goldfarb can usually walk the ten blocks from school to his home in half an hour. Today, though, he felt like running. The air seemed to be electric, with black clouds darkening the sky and a strong wind kicking up. He made it to his house in just under fifteen minutes.

As he came to his sidewalk, his father's car pulled into the driveway. Richie couldn't remember a time when his father was home before six o'clock. "Hey, you are really fast!" Richie's father, Barry, exclaimed. "I went to school to pick you up, but the bus monitor said you dashed off for home. Did you hear about the big storm?"

"No, but it sure looks like one is coming!"

"Well," his father said, "they're expecting heavy rains and maybe even a tornado. Our company just closed, along with a lot of others. Come on, let's go inside and find out the latest."

As they opened the door, Ruth Goldfarb jumped up from the hassock where she had been sitting, glued to the TV with seven-year-old Rebecca. "Oh, thank God!" she cried. "I am so glad you're both home safely. The Weather Channel has just spotted a tornado not far from here."

"Are we supposed to open up all the windows?" asked her husband. "I think we're supposed to go to the bathroom."

"No," replied Ruth. "They said on the television to get in the cellar. Let's go!"

"Shouldn't we take valuable things downstairs?" asked Barry. "What if the house gets damaged? Shouldn't we grab some photo albums or legal documents or maybe some of your jewelry?"

"Wait a minute!" shouted Rebecca. "Where is Boodles? I haven't seen her, and she must be scared. We have to go look for my cat!"

"Hey, you guys!" Richie yelled. "Listen! Can't you hear that sound? That could be the tornado!" Knowing her brother was right, Rebecca reluctantly let herself be led down the stairs.

Looking around the cellar, Ruth said, "I think we ought to go in the old coal bin. The weather man said we should go where the ceiling has the best support."

Several minutes later, they heard a sound exactly like an approaching railroad train. Two minutes after that, the house began shaking, and they felt as if they were *under* the train. Now both children were crying, and their mother fought back tears as well. Barry tried to hug and protect them all at once.

Then the roaring ended as quickly as it had begun.

"Come on," Richie urged. "We better go see how bad the damage is." He led them up the stairs and opened the door.

"You are not going to believe this," he said softly. "The house is still here. We really lucked out."

Rebecca pushed past him and ran up the stairs to her room. "Boodles! Boodles is here!"

Stunned by their good fortune that the house was not damaged, Ruth pulled a curtain aside to view the neighborhood. She saw extensive destruction, but most of the neighborhood houses were still standing.

"Yes, Richie, we really were lucky," she mused, "but I think we better come up with some kind of plan, because this could happen again. The weather has been so crazy lately. Something's going on. Maybe it's all due to that global warming. Imagine, three Category Five hurricanes in one year. We need to figure out what we're going to do in an emergency, because the next time the weather or the world goes crazy, we must have some kind of plan. Otherwise, we might not be so fortunate!"

Seen in a recent newspaper cartoon: What was the scariest costume this Halloween? Mother Nature!

There are numerous weather conditions that can be dangerous, but the four that are by far the most injurious are earthquakes, floods, hurricanes, and tornadoes. We will make recommendations for dealing with each and then follow up with some general recommendations that apply to all emergencies, such as what survival supplies to have with you.

ACTIONS TO TAKE AGAINST WEATHER EMERGENCIES

Actually, there are a number of kinds of weather emergencies, although most of us never experience them. Mudslides, extreme hot or cold temperatures, and hailstorms are examples. We have chosen to deal with the four that most people say concern them:

earthquakes, floods, hurricanes, and tornadoes. First, though, we offer recommendations that apply to all weather emergencies.

Recommendations for All Weather Emergencies

- To sign up for e-mail alerts about weather emergencies in your area, go to the following Web site: http://www.emergency emailnetwork.com.

- Prevent carbon monoxide poisoning. Carbon monoxide is an odorless, colorless gas produced by many types of equipment and is poisonous to breathe. Don't use a generator, charcoal grill, camp stove, or other gasoline- or charcoal-burning device inside your home, basement, or garage or near a window, door, or vent. Don't run a car or truck inside a garage attached to your house, even if you leave the door open. Don't heat your house with a gas oven. If your carbon monoxide detector sounds, leave your home immediately and call 911. Seek prompt medical attention if you are feeling dizzy, light-headed, or nauseated. You may have carbon monoxide poisoning.

- Pace yourself on cleanup work, and set priorities for the work that has to be done. Be alert to physical and emotional exhaustion or strain. Ask your family members, friends, or professionals for support. If needed, seek professional help.

- Prevent musculoskeletal injuries. Use teams of two or more people to move bulky objects. Avoid lifting any material that weighs more than fifty pounds (per person).

- Stay cool. When it's hot, stay in air-conditioned buildings; take breaks in shaded areas or in cool rooms; drink water and nonalcoholic fluids often; wear lightweight, light-colored, loose-fitting clothing; and do outdoor activities during cooler hours.

- Treat wounds. Clean all open wounds and cuts with soap and clean water. Apply an antibiotic ointment. Contact a doctor to find out whether more treatment is needed (such as a tetanus shot). If a wound gets red, swells, or drains, seek immediate medical attention.

- Wash your hands with soap and water. If water isn't available, you can use alcohol-based products made for washing hands.
- Wear protective gear for cleanup work: a hard hat, goggles, heavy work gloves, and watertight boots with steel toes and insoles (not just steel shank). Wear earplugs or protective headphones to reduce risk from equipment noise.

Earthquakes

Whereas California has been the state most prone to serious earthquakes in recent years, there are many other fault zones in the United States. For example, geologists and seismologists have predicted a 97 percent chance of a major earthquake in the New Madrid seismic zone of the central United States (including Arkansas, Missouri, Tennessee, and Kentucky) between now and the year 2035. While earthquakes with the power of the one that hit the greater Los Angeles area in January 1994 are fairly rare, less severe earthquakes can interrupt your normal living patterns and cause substantial injury.

What to Do to Prepare for an Earthquake

- Secure heavy furniture to the floor or walls to prevent it from falling or tipping.
- Install safety latches on the insides of drawers and cupboards to avoid items falling or breaking in the event of turbulence; place heavy or breakable objects on lower shelves.
- Identify doorways or archways that are best suited for more than one person, and practice meeting in those areas.
- Place flashlights in several rooms of the house, and check battery power regularly.

- Prepare and maintain emergency food, water, tool, and medical supplies.
- Keep flammable or hazardous materials in cabinets or secured on lower shelves.
- If your home is damaged and you make an insurance claim, you will need to prove what you have lost. Therefore, you should gather and store important documents in a fireproof safe:

    Birth certificates

    Ownership certificates (for automobiles and boats, for example)

    Social security cards

    Insurance policies

    Wills

    Household inventory, including a list of contents, photographs of contents of every room, and photographs of items of high value, such as jewelry, paintings, and collectors' items

During an Earthquake

- Get on your hands and knees under a sturdy table or desk, and clasp your hands behind the back of your neck. This is considered a safety position.
- If you're not near a table or desk, cover your face and head with your arms. Then stand or crouch in a strongly supported doorway or brace yourself in an inside corner of the house or building.
- Stay clear of windows or glass that could shatter or objects that could fall on you.
- If you are inside, stay there. Many people are injured at entrances of buildings by falling debris.

The central question most people have after an earthquake is, "Is it safe for us to go back into our house?" Here are some guidelines to answer that question.

After an Earthquake

- If your house is not still resting on its foundation, do not enter.
- If you do reenter, watch out for furniture or other heavy objects that could fall on you.
- Check for signs of fire, and listen for the hissing sound of natural gas. If you heat with oil, make sure that that system is not leaking. If you smell gas or oil, leave immediately.
- Do not use your toilet or water taps until you have been ensured that all plumbing is safe.
- Make sure your electrical system has not been compromised before plugging in any appliances. If you are unsure of their condition, call an electrician, and while you're waiting, go through the main switch on your circuit breakers.
- Look for and stay away from downed electrical lines.

Floods

You may not be aware that floods and flash floods occur in each of the fifty states. Therefore, we all live in a potential flood zone. Some statistics about floods may surprise you:

- Just an inch of water can cause costly damage to your property.
- Flash floods often bring walls of water ten to twenty feet high.
- A car can be carried away by just two feet of floodwater.
- Hurricanes, winter storms, and melting snow are common and often overlooked causes of flooding.

- New land development can increase flood risk, especially if construction changes natural runoff paths.

Insurance companies may inform people of these risks, but a few simple precautions may provide you with peace of mind and can unite your family in an effort to prepare for a flood emergency.

What to Do to Prepare for a Flood

- Contact the local county geologist or county planning department to find out if your home is located in a flash-flood-prone area or landslide-prone area.
- Learn about your community's emergency plans, warning signals, evacuation routes, and locations of emergency shelters.
- Plan and practice a flood evacuation route with your family. Ask an out-of-state relative or friend to be the family contact in case your family is separated during a flood. Make sure everyone in your family knows the name, address, and telephone number of this contact person.
- Post emergency numbers at every phone.
- Inform local authorities about any people in your family with special needs, for example, elderly or bedridden people or anyone with a disability.
- Be prepared to turn off electrical power when there is standing water, fallen power lines, or before you evacuate. Turn off gas and water supplies before you evacuate. Secure unstable building materials.
- Buy a fire extinguisher, and make sure your family knows where it is and how to use it.
- Buy and install sump pumps with battery backup power.
- Have a licensed electrician raise electric components (switches, sockets, circuit breakers, and wiring) at least one foot above your home's projected flood elevation.

- For drains, toilets, and other sewer connections, install back-flow valves or plugs to prevent floodwaters from entering.
- Anchor fuel tanks that can contaminate your basement if they are torn free. An unanchored tank outside can be swept downstream and damage other houses.

In addition to using techniques offered in the last two chapters of this book, here are FEMA's suggestions for what to do during a flood.

What to Do During a Flood

- If local authorities instruct you to do so, turn off all utilities at the main power switch, and close the main gas valve.
- If told to evacuate your home, do so immediately.
- If the waters start to rise inside your house before you have evacuated, retreat to the second floor, the attic, and, if necessary, the roof. A number of people drowned during Hurricane Katrina because the floodwaters rose above their attic level and they couldn't escape. In order to gain access to your roof, bring an axe and a saw so you can cut an adequate escape hole.
- Floodwaters may carry raw sewage, chemical waste, and other disease-spreading substances. If you've come in contact with floodwaters, wash your hands with soap and disinfected water.

After a Flood

- Identify and throw away food that may not be safe to eat, including

    Food that may have come in contact with flood or storm water

    Canned foods that are bulging, opened, or damaged

    Food that has an unusual odor, color, or texture

> Perishable foods (including meat, poultry, fish, eggs, and leftovers) that have been above 40°F for two hours or more

- Thawed food that contains ice crystals or is 40°F or below can be refrozen or cooked. If cans have come in contact with floodwater or storm water, remove the labels, wash the cans, and dip them in a solution of 1 cup of bleach in 5 gallons of water. Label cans clearly with a permanent marker.

- Store food safely. In the event of power loss, keep the refrigerator and freezer doors closed as much as possible. Add block ice or dry ice to your refrigerator if the electricity is expected to be off longer than four hours. Wear heavy gloves when handling dry ice.

- Listen to and follow public announcements. Local authorities will tell you if tap water is safe to drink or to use for cooking or bathing. If the water is not safe to use, follow local instructions to use bottled water or to boil or disinfect water for cooking, cleaning, or bathing.

- To boil or disinfect water, hold water at a rolling boil for one minute to kill bacteria. If you can't boil water, add one-eighth teaspoon (approximately 0.75 ml) of newly purchased, unscented liquid household bleach per gallon of water. Stir the water well, and let it stand for thirty minutes before you use it. You can use water-purifying tablets instead of boiling water or using bleach. For infants, use only preprepared canned baby formula. Do not use powdered formulas prepared with treated water.

- Clean children's toys that have come in contact with water. Use a solution of 1 cup of bleach in 5 gallons of water to clean the toys. Let toys air dry after cleaning.

- Avoid floodwater and mosquitoes.

- Prevent mosquito bites by wearing long pants, socks, and long-sleeved shirts and by using insect repellents that contain DEET or picaridin.

- Follow all warnings about water on roadways. Do not drive vehicles or heavy equipment through water.

- If you are caught in an area where floodwater is rising, wear a life jacket, or use some other type of flotation device.

- Clean up and prevent mold growth. Clean up and dry out the building quickly (within twenty-four to forty-eight hours). Open doors and windows. Use fans to dry out the building. To *prevent* mold growth, clean wet items and surfaces with detergent and water. To *remove* mold growth, clean with a bleach solution of 1 cup of bleach in 1 gallon of water. Be sure to wear rubber gloves, and open the windows and doors. Throw away porous items (for example, carpeting and upholstered furniture) that cannot be dried quickly. Fix any leaks in roofs, walls, or plumbing.

Hurricanes

All hurricanes are dangerous, but some are more so than others. The way storm flow, wind, and other factors combine affects a hurricane's destructive power. Here are some terms commonly used to describe hurricanes that may be helpful in preparing for an emergency:

Hurricane: A tropical cyclone in which surface winds are 74 miles per hour or greater.

Eye of the storm: The center of a tropical cyclone, surrounded by the most intense area of the storm. Inside the eye, winds are normally calm, and the sky is often clear. But once the eye passes, the wind whips around in the other direction and can be even stronger than it was before.

Hurricane watch: An announcement that hurricane conditions pose a threat to a specific area within thirty-six hours.

Hurricane warning: Hurricane force winds (74 mph or more) are expected in a specific area within twenty-four hours.

As studies by Harvard researchers of the aftermath of Hurricane Katrina show, everyone needs to be prepared to survive for three days entirely on their own ("Preparing for Disasters," 2006)!

What to Do to Prepare for a Hurricane

- Have hurricane straps installed to keep the roof attached to the walls.
- Use storm shutters to protect windows and glass from flying debris.
- If your house does not have storm shutters to protect your windows, board up windows with five-eighths-inch marine plywood. Tape will not prevent glass from breaking.
- Bring in outside furniture.
- Remove any roof antennas if you can do so safely.
- Shut off your utilities: water, electricity, and gas.
- Make sure there is gas in the car, and you are ready to evacuate immediately if you are told to do so. In virtually all areas of the country where hurricanes are likely, the government has mapped out evacuation routes. Know what yours is.

After a Hurricane

- Avoid unstable buildings and structures. Stay away from damaged buildings or structures until they have been examined and certified as safe by a building inspector or other government authority. Leave immediately if you hear shifting or unusual noises that signal that the structure is about to fall.
- Beware of wild or stray animals. Call local authorities to handle animals. Get rid of dead animals according to local guidelines.

- Beware of electrical and fire hazards. Call the power company to report fallen power lines, and NEVER touch these fallen lines. Avoid contact as well with overhead power lines during cleanup and other activities. If electrical circuits and equipment have gotten wet or are in or near water, turn off the power at the main breaker or fuse on the service panel. Do not turn the power back on until electrical equipment has been inspected by a qualified electrician. Do not burn candles near flammable items or leave any candle unattended. If possible, use flashlights or other battery-operated lights instead of candles.

- Beware of hazardous materials such as paint thinner, acid, pesticides, and gasoline. Wear protective clothing and gear (for example, a respirator if needed) when handling these materials. Wash skin that may have come in contact with hazardous chemicals. Contact local authorities if you are not sure about how to handle or get rid of hazardous materials.

Tornadoes

Knowing what to do when you see or hear a tornado warning can save your lives. A *tornado watch* is issued when weather conditions favor the formation of tornadoes, for example, during a severe thunderstorm. A *tornado warning* is issued when a tornado funnel is sighted or indicated by weather radar.

During a tornado, people face hazards from extremely high winds and risk being struck by flying and falling objects. After a tornado, the wreckage left behind poses additional injury risks. Although nothing can be done to prevent tornadoes, there are actions you can take ahead of time for your health and safety.

What to Do to Prepare for a Tornado

- When there are thunderstorms in your area, turn on your radio or TV to get the latest emergency information from local authorities. Listen for announcements of a tornado watch or tornado warning.

- Learn about the tornado warning system that your county or locality uses, and make sure everyone in the family understands it. Most tornado-prone areas have a siren system. Know how to distinguish between the siren's warnings for a tornado *watch* and a tornado *warning*.

- During a tornado watch:

    Stay tuned to local radio and TV stations or a National Oceanographic and Atmospheric Administration (NOAA) Weather Radio for further weather information.

    Watch the weather and be prepared to take shelter immediately if conditions worsen.

- Because tornadoes often accompany thunderstorms, pay close attention to changing weather conditions when there is a severe thunderstorm watch or warning.

- Keep fresh batteries and a battery-powered radio or TV on hand. Electrical power is often interrupted during thunderstorms—just when information about weather warnings is most needed.

- Take a few minutes with your family to develop a tornado emergency plan. Sketch a floor plan of your home, or walk through each room and discuss where and how to seek shelter. Show a second way to exit from each room or area. If you need special equipment such as a rope ladder, mark where it is located.

- Mark where your first-aid kit and fire extinguishers are located.

- Mark where the utility switches or valves are located so they can be turned off—if time permits—in an emergency.

- Teach your family how to administer basic first aid, how to use a fire extinguisher, and how and when to turn off water, gas, and electricity in your home.

- Learn the emergency dismissal policy for your child's school.
- Make sure your children know

  What a tornado is

  What tornado watches and warnings are

  What county or parish they live in (warnings are issued by county or parish)

  How to take shelter, whether at home or at school

FAMILY WEATHER EMERGENCY PLAN

Your family weather emergency plan should include a disaster plan and a fully supplied emergency case (the list that follows was adapted from the Federal Emergency Management Agency's suggestions at http://www.fema.gov/library/diztips.shtm):

- Decide where to go when a weather emergency occurs. This will vary depending on whether you are at home, school, work, outdoors, or in a car when a weather emergency occurs. Choose appropriate places for a flood, a severe thunderstorm or hurricane, a blizzard, and a tornado, and go there when a warning is issued. Update these plans every school year and as places of employment and residence change.
- Be sure everyone in the family knows where your family emergency supply kit (described later in this chapter) is located.
- Designate a friend or relative outside your town or area as your family contact in the event you are separated from family members during a flood or tornado, or in case a storm knocks out your electricity. Ideally this person should reside in another area of the country, one unlikely to be affected by the weather systems in your own area.
- Agree on a place where family members can meet if they are separated.

- Get a good map, and plan various evacuation routes, avoiding low-lying areas. This is especially valuable in the event of flooding from rivers, streams, tropical storms, or flash floods.

- Carry out several test runs of different routes, and select the best one, taking into account what the rest of the people in your area are likely to do.

- For times of extreme heat, if you are unable to adequately cool your domicile, identify locations where you can escape sweltering conditions for hours at a time: a mall, a movie theater, or the home of a friend or relative.

- Make sure all pets are wearing collars and up-to-date identification. Have a safe place to take your pets if possible; most disaster shelters cannot accept pets.

- Store important documents in a safety deposit box that is away from the home. You should keep valuables and copies of important papers there.

- Have a plan to get psychological help after the emergency if needed, and at the least, implement the techniques in this book to relieve the inevitable anxiety that members of your family will experience.

Take the time to assemble a fully supplied emergency case. You may need to grab it and throw it into the trunk of your car in a hurry, without any time to gather the materials you will need. Perishable items should be changed or replaced every six months. Print out this list supplied by the Federal Emergency Management Agency, and keep it handy.

Essentials

- [ ] Battery-operated radio
- [ ] Flashlight (do *not* include candles, which cause more fires after a disaster than anything else)
- [ ] Extra batteries

Water

- [ ] 3 gallons per person, minimum, in a food-grade, plastic container. If the emergency is a major one, such as Hurricane Katrina was, you will need 7 to 10 gallons of water per person. It's a lot to carry, even in your car, but you may well need it. Don't store it in the car trunk. Temperature extremes may jeopardize the water's usability.
- [ ] Additional water for sanitation

Food

- [ ] Minimum three-day supply of nonperishable food that requires no refrigeration or preparation and little or no water
- [ ] Dry cereal
- [ ] Peanut butter
- [ ] Canned fruits
- [ ] Canned vegetables
- [ ] Canned juice
- [ ] Ready-to-eat canned meats
- [ ] Ready-to-eat soups (not concentrated)
- [ ] Quick energy snacks, graham crackers
- [ ] Hand-powered can opener

First-Aid Kit (one for your home and one for each car)

- [ ] Scissors
- [ ] Sunscreen
- [ ] Thermometer

- [ ] Tweezers
- [ ] Needle
- [ ] Moistened antibacterial and alcohol towelettes
- [ ] Cleansing agent/soap
- [ ] Latex gloves (2 pairs)
- [ ] Tongue blades (2)
- [ ] Assorted sizes of safety pins
- [ ] 2-inch sterile gauze pads (4–6)
- [ ] 4-inch sterile gauze pads (4–6)
- [ ] 2-inch sterile roller bandages (3 rolls)
- [ ] 3-inch sterile roller bandages (3 rolls)
- [ ] Triangular bandages (3)
- [ ] Tube of petroleum jelly or other lubricant
- [ ] Sterile adhesive bandages in assorted sizes

Nonprescription Drugs

- [ ] Laxatives
- [ ] Antidiarrhea medication
- [ ] Aspirin or nonaspirin pain reliever
- [ ] Antacid (for stomach upset)
- [ ] Activated charcoal (use if advised by the Poison Control Center)
- [ ] Syrup of Ipecac (use to induce vomiting if advised by the Poison Control Center)

Tools and Supplies

- [ ] Whistle
- [ ] Aluminum foil
- [ ] Crowbar
- [ ] Compass
- [ ] Paper, pencil
- [ ] Plastic sheeting
- [ ] Medicine dropper
- [ ] Needles, thread

- ☐ Signal flare
- ☐ Matches in a waterproof container
- ☐ Assorted nails, wood screws
- ☐ Pliers, screwdriver, hammer
- ☐ Plastic storage containers
- ☐ Heavy cotton or hemp rope
- ☐ Cash or traveler's checks, change
- ☐ Map of the area (for locating shelters)
- ☐ Nonelectric can opener, utility knife
- ☐ Mess kits, or paper cups, plates, and plastic utensils
- ☐ Tape, duct and plumber's tape or strap iron
- ☐ Patch kit and can of seal-in-air for tires
- ☐ Shut-off wrench, to turn off household gas and water

Sanitation

- ☐ Disinfectant
- ☐ Household chlorine bleach
- ☐ Soap, liquid detergent
- ☐ Personal hygiene items
- ☐ Feminine supplies
- ☐ Plastic bucket with tight lid
- ☐ Toilet paper, towelettes, paper towels
- ☐ Plastic garbage bags, ties (for personal sanitation uses)

Clothing and Bedding

- ☐ Sunglasses
- ☐ Rain gear
- ☐ Hat and gloves
- ☐ Sturdy shoes or work boots
- ☐ Blankets or sleeping bags
- ☐ Thermal underwear
- ☐ One complete change of clothing and footwear per person

For Babies

- [ ] Formula
- [ ] Diapers
- [ ] Bottles
- [ ] Medication
- [ ] Powdered milk

For Pets

- [ ] Food
- [ ] Water
- [ ] No-spill food and water containers
- [ ] Identification number and central registry phone number for pets that are microchipped
- [ ] Records of vaccinations
- [ ] Leash, harness, or carrier

Family Documents

- [ ] Important telephone numbers
- [ ] Record of bank account numbers
- [ ] Family records (birth, marriage, death certificates)
- [ ] Inventory of valuable household goods
- [ ] Copy of will, insurance policies, contracts, deeds, stocks and bonds
- [ ] Record of credit card account numbers and companies
- [ ] Copy of passports, social security cards, immunization records

Family Medical Needs

- [ ] Insulin
- [ ] Prescription drugs
- [ ] Denture needs
- [ ] Extra eyeglasses
- [ ] Contact lenses and supplies
- [ ] Heart and high blood pressure medication

Entertainment

Books, playing cards, paper, pens, crayons; for a child's survival kit, go to http://www.fema.gov/kids/k_srvkit.htm

Pets and Livestock

For tips for saving pets and livestock, go to this FEMA Web site: www.fema.gov/library/diztips.shtm

Special tip: Jon Robertson has written a book that is loaded with ideas about "how to eat well when the power goes out." Creatively entitled *Apocalypse Chow* (2005), this treasure trove of cooking ideas would have been helpful reading for those caught in the recent spate of weather emergencies. There's even a chapter on how to prepare a hot meal on your car's engine block when you're stuck in a massive traffic jam.

❧

You may be thinking that this is an exceedingly long list of recommendations, and it is. Certainly you should use your own judgment about what to do or include. In the past, it probably wouldn't have been worth it to go to all this trouble, but with the trend toward more violent weather, it is probably now a reasonable goal.

3

KIDNAPPING

"Don't Go Anywhere Without Me!"

The following story was written by Maureen, a fifty-five-year-old woman, about a time when she was almost kidnapped. It illustrates the rejection children can feel when they aren't believed. Why do so many parents disbelieve their kids when told that they have narrowly escaped danger?

SHE WOULDN'T BELIEVE ME!

When I was growing up, my mother used to go to the grocery store virtually every day and would often leave one or another of us kids in the car in a parking lot in our "safe" suburban town. One summer day when I was about five, I came close to being kidnapped from that parking lot. A middle-aged couple approached our car, looking purposeful and nervous in their dark glasses, and spoke to me through the window, which was open on that hot afternoon.

"Would you like to go out for ice cream with us?" asked the woman brightly, with a smile that looked pasted on.

Yikes, I thought, *these people could be kidnappers!*

"No," I said, looking straight ahead. "I need to wait here for my mother."

"Oh, we'll bring you right back! Don't you *like* ice cream, little girl?" persisted the woman.

I noticed both of them kept glancing around the parking lot.

"I have to wait here for my mother," I repeated, "but thank you anyway." I smiled weakly, figuring I should err on the side of politeness with these bad people. They wouldn't force me to go with them, would they?

"Well, if that's what you really want to do!" the woman huffed, her fake smile gone now. The couple walked away quickly, eyes darting left and right.

A few minutes later when my mother came back with her grocery bags, I blurted out the whole story to her. She looked startled as she listened to my tale. "Should we tell the police, or Dad, or both?" I asked her.

Mom paused a moment before turning to me, her face composed once again. I remember her exact words: "If what you said really happened, you did the right thing."

"Of course it really happened!" I screamed at her. "They must have been kidnappers!" My outrage was tempered with a touch of pride: at least she said I had done the right thing.

Mom made that "pipe down" motion with her hand. "If it's true, it's over and done with now, and nothing we need to concern Dad with, and certainly not the police." She made it clear that this was the end of the story.

A few years later, when my younger brother was about four and I was around eight, we were walking by ourselves to the town library. It was about a half-mile from our house, and much of the journey was along a wooded path and under a railroad trestle bridge. As we came up to the bridge, a young man was standing next to the path, facing away from us, and yet he was watching us intently over his shoulder. Curious, I looked back a few times as we passed him. He remained on that spot, staring at us, holding something in front of his pants.

"Why is he watching us? What is he doing?" my little brother asked, clearly both curious and yet alarmed even at his age.

"He's just holding a hot dog," I told my brother, improvising a placating lie. It wasn't until years later that I realized the man was masturbating and being aroused by watching children.

"We better tell Mom, right?" He looked up at me with concern and trust, and I didn't hesitate with my answer: "No, we'll just hurry along and ignore him. Silly man! We're almost at the library now, and we can walk home a different way."

We never did tell either of our parents. I have no way of knowing if that couple in the parking lot ever did kidnap a child (or worse) or if that man near the railroad bridge ever did molest a child (or worse). I only know I still feel angry at my mother for making me feel I couldn't trust her enough to tell her about this scary experience. In fact, I really don't trust authority figures in general, and I can't help thinking that this is why.

THE EXTENT OF THE PROBLEM

Of the nearly 1 million missing persons reported each year, 80 percent are children. Of course, many of them are not kidnapped but merely lost. Nevertheless, most parents dread the thought of abduction, for two reasons: they fear for the safety and quick return of their child and feel that if their child is abducted, they must be responsible in some way. No matter how well they may provide for the child's well-being, they feel that if they had done a better job, the kidnapping wouldn't have happened. This probably also explains why they sometimes doubt their children's stories of threatened or actual abuse. For most of us, both feelings are unspeakably awful. A new national survey commissioned by Honeywell Corp. learned that kidnapping is the number two safety concern among parents and grandparents. The study also revealed an alarming lack of information about child safety resources and prevention strategies.

Abduction by Family Members

Of the 200,000 children who are kidnapped by family members each year, 99 percent are found within hours or days by the usual law enforcement response. Ninety-one percent are returned alive and unharmed. Six percent are located but not returned. Family abductions are defined as "the taking or keeping of a child by a family member in violation of a custody order, a decree, or other legitimate custodial rights, where the taking or keeping involved some element of concealment, flight, or intent to deprive a lawful custodian indefinitely of custodial privileges." For children ages fifteen to eighteen, the family member must have used some kind of force or threat in order for the event to be considered abduction (unless the child is mentally disabled). A family member is defined as a biological, foster, or genetic relative; the partner of a family member or parent; or someone who acts on behalf of a family member.

Not surprisingly, the majority of family child abductions occur within families that have experienced a divorce or separation, where the child is living with only one parent. In terms of gender and racial/ethnic differences, family child abductions occur proportionately as groups do in the population at large. The biological father is responsible for half of all abductions, and the biological mother is responsible for about a quarter. Most kidnappings occur from the child's own home or yard (36 percent) or from someone else's home or yard (37 percent). Removal from day care or school is relatively infrequent (only 7 percent). Children are kidnapped from the other venues—public area, parent's or caretaker's car, on the street, or while on vacation—less than 10 percent of the time each.

The use of threat, force, or any kind of weapon is extremely rare in family child abductions. The more common causes for these abductions include taking the child with the intent to prevent the other primary caregiver from further contacting the child (76 percent) and abducting the child with the intent to affect custody permanently (82 percent). Two-thirds of the time, the child was in the custody of the abductor when the kidnapping happened. Although kidnappings are most likely to happen in summer and least likely in spring, there really isn't much difference between the seasons.

Abduction by Nonfamily Members

In 2000, there were about sixty thousand child abductions by persons other than family members. These children were moved using physical force or detained for at least one hour in a place of isolation. They were taken for the purposes of ransom, concealment, or of being kept permanently.

Only about 7 percent of the abducted children were five years old or younger. In fact, the older the child, the greater the odds were of being abducted: six to eleven years old, 12 percent; twelve to fourteen years old, 22 percent; and fifteen to seventeen years old, 59 percent. Twice as many girls as boys are victims. Whites account for 33 percent of all nonfamily abductees, African Americans for 42 percent, and Latinos, 25 percent.

About two-thirds of the victims of kidnappings are girls. Half of all nonfamily abductions that occur involve perpetrators who are known by the child. Most of them are friends or long-term acquaintances. Only about 5 percent of the total are neighbors, and only 4 percent of perpetrators are caretakers or baby-sitters. The rest are strangers, 80 percent of whom work alone and most of whom are between twenty and twenty-nine years old.

Many children (one-third) taken by nonfamily members were walking down the street or sitting in a car. The second most dangerous place is a park or wooded area (one-quarter). About one-fifth happen when the child is playing in someone else's yard, and although many mothers worry most about in the family yard and school or day care, less than 5 percent actually occur in those places. Children kidnapped by nonfamily members are missing for two hours or less about a third of the time, and another 60 percent are gone for no longer than one day.

ACTIONS TO TAKE AGAINST KIDNAPPING

So what are the implications of these data on kidnapping? What do they tell you about what steps you can reasonably take to protect your own kids? Some of the suggestions we make might surprise you.

THE INNOCENT-LOOKING WHITE VAN

Maureen De Salvo can't take her eyes off the TV program on child abduction. The mother of three-year-old Timothy, Maureen worries constantly that someone will kidnap him. The documentary film she is watching begins with an ordinary scene on a summer evening. A young mother crosses a parking lot, walks up to her station wagon, and opens the back door. Hanging from one arm is a cloth shopping bag, and on the other is a baby car seat with her smiling seven-month-old baby in it. The camera focuses briefly on a white van beside her, apparently unoccupied.

She puts the bag on the ground while she places the car seat in the back of the vehicle. As she reaches for the safety belt for the car seat, her car is struck softly in the rear. Startled, she backs out of the car and walks around to see what has happened. As she does so, the other vehicle reverses and, without a word of apology, speeds toward the lot entrance. "Hey," the woman yells at the retreating vehicle, "you just hit my car! Wait a minute!"

While she is preoccupied, the side door of the van opens, a man jumps out, and he rapidly moves to her car. Reaching in, he grabs the baby and the car seat and ducks back into his van with them. He slams the door, turns on the engine, and races away. The mother stands frozen with one hand leaning on the trunk, her face distorted in horror.

"What should this young mother have done differently?" the TV commentator intones. "When she saw that the van was parked along the driver's side of her car, she should have entered it from the passenger side, just in case."

"She never should have parked in that lot in the first place," Maureen thinks to herself. "Not with a young kid at night. Most parking lots are crawling with creepy people. I know I'm never going to park in one again!"

What do you think? Is Maureen overreacting, or is she simply being reasonable?

Our suggestions on how to avoid a kidnapping are organized into four categories: general tips and tips for infants, children, and teens.

General Tips

- If you return to your car in a parking lot and find a van has parked next to the driver's side, go around and get in the passenger's side, locking all the doors as you do. Recently abductors have taken to springing out of the side of the van just as their victim is unlocking her car, dragging her back into the van, and immobilizing her. The operation takes only seconds, and they can be gone before anyone even notices. They may also use this technique to grab a child from your arms or sometimes just to carjack the car itself.

- If after you have started your car, you notice a flyer taped to your back window, do not get out to remove it. Drive to another place before doing so. Abductors wait until you go to the back of the car; then they slip into the passenger's side. When you return, they force you to drive wherever they want.

- More abductions occur in June, July, and August than at any other time, so be especially alert during the summer months.

- Help your children to identify adults in their lives who can be trusted. Such adults should be able to act effectively if one of your children tells them about suspicious behavior by another adult (or teen). Encourage your children to report any such suspicious behavior to you or, if you're not immediately available, to one of these adults.

- Your child should understand that although new situations can be exciting and fun, there is also the possibility of danger. They will need to be a little more vigilant than usual when they are in unfamiliar surroundings.

- Know all of your children's friends and their families if you possibly can.

- If you possibly can, know where your child is, and with whom, at all times.

- Young children should always be accompanied to school by an adult. Older children should walk to school in groups.

- Make sure your school will always notify you immediately if your child is absent.

- Your children's schools should maintain a list of those people who are authorized to pick them up.

- Teach your child to let you know if some new person is paying a lot of attention to him or her.

- Do not force your child to be left alone with anyone he or she does not want to be left with. Children often have better intuitions about such situations than you do.

- Be sure that your children know that if they become separated from you while shopping, they should go to the nearest clerk or security person and ask for help.

- Keep up-to-date photographs and a medical and dental history of each of your children. It is also a good idea to have your children fingerprinted. If your police department keeps a file on area children, insert these data into the file.

- While at the police station, look at the Megan's Law CD. This CD details the identity and residence of convicted sex offenders who may live in or around your community. In many states, you can now get this information online.

- Try to remember what clothes your children are wearing each day.

- Do not put your child's name on clothing or belongings where strangers can see the name.

- Have a code word you use if you need someone to give a message to your child. If the messenger is unable to supply the code word to your children, they should never go away with the person.

- Tell your children to always run away from danger. If they feel scared, they should run away. They shouldn't be afraid to make a scene by yelling for help. They should not worry about being polite or be afraid of being a tattletale when it comes to safety. Any misunderstanding can be cleared up later.

- Do not assume that other family members or friends watch your child with the same diligence as you. Your child's grandmother, for instance, grew up in an era when children were not abducted with the frequency they are today.

Tips for Infants

- If you are having a baby, choose, if at all possible, a hospital that has placed video cameras in nurseries monitored by staff. It is also safer if staff place bracelets on newborn babies containing computerized chips that broadcast an alarm when the baby is moved from the location. In addition, check the IDs of nurses too, since they change shifts frequently.

- Sometimes parents of infants are caught off guard by strangers who ask, "Can I hold your baby?" This is an inappropriate request and should always be answered firmly but politely: "Now is not a good time, thank you."

- Be sure your baby's auto seat is firmly attached so that it cannot be removed easily.
- Never leave a baby alone in a car for even a few seconds.

Tips for Children

- Never force your children to kiss or embrace anyone. If you do, they will learn that they ought to do it even when they don't feel like it. Seducers often use guilt feelings in children to achieve their illicit goals.
- Tell your children that secrets can be fun but too often can lead to trouble. Otherwise they may be convinced that keeping secrets from you is okay.
- Teach your children that although most people are safe, there might be bad people in your area who would do them harm if they could.
- Explain to your child how kidnappers often try to convince children that their parents do not want them. Explain that this is a trick they use to keep the children from trying to contact anyone.
- Arrange with neighbors on your child's route to school to put a sign in their window saying, "Safe Home." Teach your child that these are houses where they should go if they experience suspicious behavior.
- Make sure each of your children knows their phone number and that they ought to call 911 in an emergency. Show them how to use a pay phone even if they have no money. Cell phones can be programmed with parents' or others' numbers, and children can be shown how to access these numbers.
- When you are with your children in a crowd, agree on a place to go in case you become separated.
- Teach your children to recognize suspicious behavior. For example, they should know not to go with someone who asks for help finding a lost puppy.

- We used to tell children that "stranger = danger." This message does not apply so much anymore. Children are actually more likely to be victimized by someone you or they know. Children get very confused by the "stranger" idea, and sometimes it scares them to the point of refusing to talk to anyone outside family and friends.

- The media are rife with reports of children being abducted from public areas such as playgrounds while their parents read or chatted with others. Unlike earlier times, today you really do need to pay attention. If you are taking two or three children to the playground and if one were to skin a knee, call the other children over to "help" so that you maintain watch over the entire group.

- Public restrooms are another venue where parents should exercise caution with their children. No matter what the child's sex, take your child with you into the bathroom.

Tips for Teens

- Make sure that your teenaged children receive age-appropriate sex education. If the school doesn't do it (and most don't), check to see if a religious organization that is acceptable to you offers such training. If not, learn to do the job yourself. Children who do not understand the basics of sex are much more easily seduced and abducted.

- Show your children missing-child bulletins, and discuss the circumstances under which those children went missing.

- Keeping with the adage, "There is safety in numbers," teens should be advised not to go to places alone. They should always try to take a friend, even to go jogging in the neighborhood.

- Collect all of your children's friend's phone numbers, so that you can contact them readily if one of your children becomes missing.

- Stress to your teens that they must not ride with anyone they do not know. Anyone offering a ride unexpectedly—even a family friend—should have been given the family code word in advance.

Kidnapping may be the most frightening threat to most parents, but we hope you can see that the big picture is not nearly so dire as the media sometimes present. With these precautions, your children should be absolutely safe.

4

TERRORISM

"How Are We Supposed to Know What to Do?"

Your children may be more aware of the possibility of a terrorist attack than you think. However, their understanding is seldom accurate enough to properly deal with their feelings about this threat. Children can sense parents' uneasiness and may become confused when their parents do not communicate their own feelings. Often parents can have a hard time finding a balance between sharing their own feelings with their children and not passing their anxiety on to their children. You will need to confront your own emotions before you can begin to help your children process theirs.

Watching the news together (avoiding disturbing graphics) is a good opportunity to discuss your children's attitudes toward the issues. There are many other actions you can take to help them handle the emotional impact of terrorism, as well as to protect their safety. Some of the recommendations you will hear about from friends may be ill advised, however, and we will warn you against these ideas too.

ACTIONS TO TAKE AGAINST TERRORISM

The single most important thing you can do to protect your children from the very remote possibility of involvement in a terrorist attack is to have a discussion with them about what precautions they need to take as they live their lives. Here's what to say and do.

How to Talk to Your Children About Terrorism

- Experts suggest that you should ask children over seven years old what they know and think about terrorism and the likelihood of an attack. It is helpful to have an understanding of how aware of terrorism your children are and how accurate their information is. Ask them what they have learned from television, newspapers, and magazines and what they have heard from others. It may surprise you to hear that they have had many discussions with peers and others on this topic.

- In general, convey two messages to your children: that you will do everything in your power to keep them safe and that the government is doing everything in its power to keep the country safe. Explain that many men and women—brave police officers, firefighters, doctors, and soldiers, among many others—work every day to keep us safe.

- Stay close to your children emotionally and physically. Your presence is comforting and reassuring.

- Encourage your children to ask questions. An environment that fosters open dialogue is important. Talk specifically about what frightens them. Make it clear to them that there is nothing they need to hold back. You are there to listen and support them.

- Your instruction about what to do in the event of terrorism should be brief, simple, and reassuring.

- Tell the truth. Try your best not to minimize or exaggerate, but tailor your responses appropriately. Younger children need to understand it is most unlikely that "bad people will try to harm them." Older children can be involved in more in-depth discussions and can participate in making suggestions about how to make society safe. They should think about how to make their schools and neighborhoods safer, and how they think tragedies like 9/11 could be prevented. Discussions with older children can help them feel empowered and therefore less afraid.

- Make a judgment of how sensitive each of your children is. Realize that the more fearful they are, the more careful you are going to have to be in handling the situation.

- Some parents think that the use of force is always a bad idea: everyone should try to use words to resolve our conflicts. Others may believe that at times, fighting is the right thing to do when words have failed. It is important for you and your partner to discuss your opinions on this sometimes delicate subject. Teens may be included in this discussion, especially if you want them to come to their own conclusions. It may not be a good idea to present young children with competing points of view.

- Always try to foster a family environment that encourages the expression of thoughts and feelings. Your children are getting lots of information from others. Make sure they are getting accurate information from you.

Keeping Your Children Safe from Terrorism

- Devise a family emergency plan in the event of a terrorist attack. The Emergency Action Questionnaire presented later in this chapter will help your family do this.

- Maintain normal routines as much as possible in the event of a scare. This will help to ensure your children's sense of safety and serenity.

- Check with your children's schools to see what they are discussing in the classroom about terrorism.

- Find out if your children's schools have plans in place for emergency situations. Urge them to create such plans if they have not already done so.

- Ask your family doctor's opinion about getting yourself and your family a smallpox vaccination.

- Have an emergency supply of cash readily available. Going to the bank during an emergency may be impossible.

- Take a good first-aid course.

After you have done most or all of these things, your children may still be seriously concerned about terrorism. If you have already tried the anxiety-reducing methods described in this book and their fears continue to disturb their daily activities, sleeping or eating habits, or behavior, you should consult a mental health professional. And remember that the most important thing you can do for your children is to get a grip on your own fears because this will translate into an atmosphere of safety in your home.

WHAT NOT TO DO ABOUT TERRORISM

There are several other actions you may hear about that experts agree are unwarranted and may even serve to further alarm you and your family. Here's what they suggest:

- Don't build a bomb shelter.
- Don't seal a room in your house to prepare for chemical warfare.
- Don't restrict your travel plans or your attendance at large public events due to fear of terrorists, unless warned by authorities to do so.
- Don't make promises you cannot keep. For instance, you cannot promise your children that there will not be a war, but you can promise that you will always do your best to keep them safe.

KAY'S KIDS AND THE LONDON SUBWAY ATTACKS
When Kay Turner's children, Alex, fifteen, and Celia, twelve, watched the news films of the London subway terrorist attacks

in the summer of 2005, they were confused about what had happened and why.

"Why would anyone want to kill innocent people, no matter how mad they are?" Alex asked Kay.

"Are most Arabs like that?" Celia wanted to know. "Do we need to stay away from them in this country too?"

"Do you think the subway here in Boston is safe? Where are they likely to hit next?" Alex wondered.

Kay felt overwhelmed. She was sure that not all Arabs are bad people, but as to the children's other questions, she didn't know the answers. Then an idea struck her: "Listen, kids, let's do what we usually do when we need other kinds of information. Let's look on the Internet."

She "Asked Jeeves" (www.askjeeves.com) this question: "What should I tell children about terrorism?" The first site she found assured her that "talking about violent acts with teens should actually decrease their fears. Having children keep scared feelings to themselves is more damaging than open discussion. As with other topics, consider the child's age and level of understanding when entering into a discussion."

Kay was advised to refrain from lecturing or teaching about the issues until there had been some exploration about what is most important, confusing, or troublesome to the children. The site also urged that she not force a discussion on her children if they showed signs of not being ready for it, for example, by their facial expressions or changing the subject.

Kay found that she could use such far-off violent events as the mayhem in London to stimulate a discussion of nonviolent problem solving for issues closer to home. For instance, she could compare the tactics terrorists used for resolving a dispute to the methods her children use to resolve their own disagreements.

Finally, the site recommended that she space such discussions out so that the children do not become overwhelmed by the information or its ramifications. Everyone needs time to process such emotionally laden data. Several brief talks are better than one long one.

THE EMERGENCY ACTION QUESTIONNAIRE

We often hear it said that a crisis brings out the best in people. That's what we would all like to think, but studies show that emergencies evoke the best *and* the worst, depending on the person. Most people are at their best only when they have strong emotional supports—a loving spouse, close friends, a cohesive family. This is true whether the emergency is local (a fire breaks out next door), regional (a winter storm cripples transportation), national (commercial flights are being shot down), or universal (international war is being waged among nuclear powers).

Here is an activity that will foster cohesion in your family by helping them:

- Become more aware of their emotional reactions.
- Learn that they are not alone in their concerns.
- Brainstorm possible family plans and choose the best one in preparation for a potential crisis.
- Support each other in carrying out the plan.

Families that are able to act effectively together during an emergency not only protect themselves but also serve as excellent models for everyone else.

Many children are prepared for the more common emergencies: they know when to call 911 and at which neighbor's house to meet if they are forced out of their home. But there are unusual emergencies that occur and require more specialized knowledge. Long-term loss of electricity on a wide area, as happened in the northeastern United States in 1965; widespread flooding; terrorism; crippling storms; violent threats of injury during home invasion: the list goes on and on. Sometimes children think erroneously that they can handle these kinds of problems on their own too. What is needed is a detailed plan to handle almost any emergency.

Jacques and Danielle D'Estang came up with what was quite a good technique for helping their family cope not only with the threats they might have to face, but with their feelings about those threats. To avoid unnecessarily frightening their two daughters, twelve-year-old Valerie and eight-year-old Simone, the D'Estangs carried this exercise out in a nonthreatening situation.

They picked a pleasant sunny morning and met in the room in their house in which a number of windows could be opened to fresh outdoor aromas. They played soothing music and put some fragrant flowers in the room. They used their most serene and reassuring voices in explaining what their two girls were to do. They sat on the floor with the children and asked them to help draw up a list of all the emergencies and tragedies that the family might encounter. The parents knew that their children's participation would be vital in this process. From this larger list, they decided to make a more detailed checklist designed to prepare for the interruption of electricity and water as the result of terrorist action. As they were brainstorming what they would need, they realized that their list had to be differentiated in order to include items according to age.

For example, eight-year-old Simone was concerned about such worries as having strangers come into her house and getting burned while trying to light matches. Her older sister pointed to the likelihood that some anxious people would become angry and aggressive, or could turn to alcohol and drugs to calm themselves and then try to drive. The whole family would be upset about their inability to obtain safe food and water supplies during an extended power outage. When their list of concerns was completed, they used the Emergency Action Questionnaire (see Exhibit 4.1), which Danielle had found on the Internet, to organize their response.

EXHIBIT 4.1. Emergency Action Questionnaire

On a separate sheet of paper, describe the hypothetical crisis situation. Then write out your family's answers to the following items:

1. Whom do we all call if we become separated from one another? (It is probably wise that everyone call someone such as the children's grandparents if they live far enough away so as not to be affected by whatever crisis you're dealing with.) Where is our family meeting place if this problem happens? Who are the people you can trust if you are out of contact with our family when this happens? Under what conditions should we dial 911?

2. What action should you take if you are injured in this situation? If another member of the family is hurt?

3. What kind of materials should we keep in the house in case this kind of emergency should occur? [A set of recommended supplies may be found in Chapter Two.]

4. Are there any books, articles, or videotapes that can help us to prepare for this type of difficulty?

5. What Web sites would be useful to help us prepare?

6. Is there anyone we know who could give us some good advice about how to deal with a problem like this?

7. Can we design some kind of activity, something that will help to keep us all calm, that we can use when we find ourselves faced with this kind of crisis? Remember that no matter how disruptive the situation may appear, after a period of inconvenience it is almost certainly going to turn out all right.

Copy your answers to these questions and any others you can think of for everyone in your family (and any other friends and relatives you may want to share your ideas with). From time to time, take out one of the questionnaire answer sheets, and use it as a pop quiz. Danielle made a contest out of answering the questions. The odds that the D'Estangs will ever need to use this material are slight, but at least now they can feel ready.

෨ඌ

Terrorism is probably the concern most likely to cause people to overreact and overprepare. Experts say that even if a dirty nuclear device were set off in a city, it is likely to affect only a few blocks. Therefore, this is a worry that you might better deal with by carrying out the antianxiety activities described in Chapters Ten and Eleven.

5

INAPPROPRIATE MEDIA INFLUENCE

"Why Do They Keep Showing That Same Awful Scene?"

You might be surprised at how much television and media exposure our children face these days. For instance, a survey of those eight to eighteen years old by the Kaiser Family Foundation in 2006 found that the total amount of media content the average child is exposed to has gone up by more than one hour over the past five years, to eight and a half hours each day. Many studies show the negative effects that excessive television watching may have on children: increased probability of difficulty in school, more aggressive behavior, and unhealthy influence on weight. Overexposure to TV can be damaging to children at all stages of development.

There is also evidence of negative effects of refusing to allow them to watch. For example, that may cause an inability to relate to friends about this central subject of conversation. Also, strict limitations on television can lead to excessive viewing when parents aren't watching. What should you do?

THE MEDIA LITERACY APPROACH

Media literacy means increasing the understanding of media by parents, teachers, and children. Teaching children more about television, the Internet, video games, pornography, and violent music can increase their resistance to negative influences. Such an education must include the methodology, programming, content, technology, and economics of modern media.

The media literacy approach accepts that children will be exposed to a number of inappropriate concepts, especially lewd sexuality and violence, and it teaches them how to censor and understand their own viewing. Hence, it takes a different tack from other popular programs such as zero tolerance. When children become media literate, they will be less susceptible to the potential negative effects. Here's what advocates of media literacy urge you to do:

- It is unreasonable to think that shutting off the television entirely will protect and shelter your children from everything harmful in the world. In fact, this will probably lead to inappropriate exposure to media in other ways, at times when you are not watching and they have no one to discuss it with. Harshly restricting exposure is not the answer.

- Reward the realization that scenes on television and in the movies are not real. Your children will be more critical and better able to differentiate reality from fantasy. They will then be able to think about what they are watching and make decisions on their own about what to watch.

- Help your children to differentiate between the values expressed by television and those your family espouses. Have them compare stereotypical roles of minorities and women on television and their own experiences with minorities and women. They will be able to make more meaningful judgments in the future.

- Point out how technology is used to influence viewers' values and preferences.

- Emphasize that the audience has a role in media. Encourage your children to write to television shows or channels and express their opinions.

- Monitor their play, and encourage imaginative play rather than rote imitation of media roles, such as violent war games.

Pose questions to deemphasize black-and-white concepts such as good and bad, and make your children more aware of the gray area between these concepts.

- Pay attention to the television ratings system, and teach your child about it. Many channels show a rating for fifteen seconds at the beginning of a show that indicates which age group the show is intended for. Children may respond very well to the important job of looking at the ratings and restricting themselves to only watching shows that you approve of.

- Consider using the V-chip. V-chip technology allows a parent to program the television to obstruct viewing on certain shows based on their content. Most televisions made after July 1, 2000, have V-chip technology. The majority of parents, however, are unaware that this is available.

- Try to be there when your child is watching television, surfing the Net, or otherwise interacting with media. Watching television with your children is an important aspect in improving your own and their media literacy. By discussing the shows that you watch together, they will better understand what they see and can make appropriate judgments.

ACTIONS TO TAKE AGAINST INAPPROPRIATE MEDIA INFLUENCES

Although inappropriate media influence is ubiquitous, there are quite a few defenses you can employ.

The Internet

As with television, protecting your children from getting hurt on the Internet means teaching them to be responsible for their actions. One of the most important things to emphasize is that the behaviors they engage in online should reflect how they behave in real life. This is a good way for children to become their own judges in determining which online behaviors are appropriate.

Children also need to understand the public nature of the Internet. Although the Internet seems less personal than a face-to-face interaction, someone is still on the receiving end of their choices even though he or she cannot be seen. Even in casual communication, it is important to consider whether the receiving party will be able to accurately interpret the intended tone of a message or will possibly become upset. Conversely, they should not react too quickly or strongly to something that they see or read on the Internet. They should take a few minutes away from the computer to calm down and carefully interpret the situation before reacting. Here's what you should do to ensure their safety.

Protecting Your Computer

- Install spyware and adware blocking software on your computer.

- Install antivirus software, and update it regularly.

- Make sure you have a working firewall.

- Take advantage of spam-blocking tools offered by your Internet provider or e-mail software.

- Learn and use filtering and parental control technologies. Block everything that isn't preapproved rather than just filtering out the "bad" sites.

- Use a pop-up blocker or toolbar (like Google's).

- Make sure that you control the family account password, and know your children's passwords too. Lock your private files with a password they don't know. Change all passwords often.

- Do not open e-mail attachments that you are not expecting. There has been a rapid increase in viruses infecting entire computer systems.

- Resist the urge to "unsubscribe" to junk e-mail. Any response at all triggers more junk e-mail. Your response, in effect, confirms that your e-mail address is a valid one.

- Install computer updates when available.

Recommended Rules for Children When They Are Online

- Think before you fire off that witty remark. Will the person on the other end know when you are joking?

- Follow the golden rule of cyberspace: Don't do anything online that you wouldn't do in real life.

- Walk away from the computer and "take five" before responding to something that upsets you online.

- Avoid spreading rumors, assisting in "cyberbullying," or sharing private communications online.

- Bookmark your favorite Web sites so you won't mistype them and end up at a "bad" site.

- Make good use of search engines such as Yahooligans and Ask.com.

- If you are playing an online interactive game such as X-Box Live or Sony Playstation network, try to know who you are playing with.

- Make sure that you understand what information should or shouldn't be shared online. Get your parent's permission before posting any content, including profiles and blogs, to a Web site or sending it via e-mail or instant messaging. Cell phone numbers should never be posted online; the wrong people can access them.

- Although media piracy is possible, it is stealing. Get an account with iTunes or some other legal music download site.

- To learn online safety, check out wiredkids.org or internetsuperheroes.org. Consider setting up a teenangels.org chapter or starting an online safety club at your school. (Visit internetsuperheroes.org for free materials.)

- Help keep your younger brothers and sisters safe online.

- Not all the information on the Internet is true. Be sure to check your sources.

Recommended Computer Rules for Parents

- Consider keeping the computer in a public area of the house, such as the family room, so that you can be better aware of all computer activities and offer help if needed.

- Think about whether your children really need e-mail or instant messaging. If you decide that they do, block all communications from anyone other than preapproved senders.

- Make sure that you know (in real life) everyone on their "buddy list."

- Establish online time limits, and stick to them unless one of your children has a special project for school.

- Check with their teachers often for suggested Web sites and for recommendations for good resources online.

- Look for safe site lists you can trust. For instance, check out WiredKids.org's safe sites list.

- Sit down with your kids as often as possible, and find out where they go online and what they like. Discuss options that you disapprove of.

- Consider using monitoring software to be able to review what Internet sites your children have been visiting.

- Occasionally use a search engine to look for their names, screen names, address, and telephone numbers to make sure there isn't information available that you don't want on the Internet. Older children can do this themselves.

- Occasionally browse your computer for images, music, movie, media, or word files you don't know about. Check the download manager to see what is being downloaded.

- Block your older children from accessing social networks or online dating sites such as xanga.com, friendster.com, or match.com.

- Buy daughters a copy of *A Girl's Life Online* (formerly known as "Katie.com"; Tarbox, 2004).

- Be familiar with any of the programs that your child is using. Don't trust descriptions on the package; take a tour of the software yourself. Also, there are Web sites that describe and review software (see the appendix at the end of the book), where you can get a clearer view of what is on the disk.

- Because identities on the Internet are easily forged, always be wary of false identities. Discontinue any suspicious activities.

- Although video games, cell phones, instant messaging, iPods, and other high-tech gear are part of growing up in a digital world, excessive use of them can have deleterious effects on your children. It's not easy, but you need to get an assessment of the total amount of time they are spending on these technologies. If it seems to be unreasonable to you, take steps to reduce use.

- Remind your kids that you're around if they need your help.

Video Games

As with other media sources, video games can have negative and positive effects on children. Like most other media, the content of the game is much more important than any inherent characteristics of video itself. Some studies have found that video games, especially fantasy games like Myst and simulation games like Sim City and Flight Simulator, offer important benefits: better cognitive skills, the ability to plan ahead, increased visual-spatial abilities, better

hand-eye coordination, and greater attention to detail. Another positive aspect of video games is the more active nature of the games
themselves, as opposed to movies and television, which are passive.
Video games also give children a sense of accomplishment. Players
are often motivated to continue using video games without any
extrinsic rewards. They enjoy playing and getting to the next level
simply for its own sake. In those respects, children profit from enjoying video games.

A U.S. surgeon general's report (American Psychological Association, 2006b) found that children who regularly view cruelty may
become less sensitive to the pain and suffering of others, more fearful of the world around them, and more likely to behave in aggressive or harmful ways toward others. In rare cases, such viewing has
even produced physiological effects like seizures. Another almost
unsettling drawback has come to the light with the game Grand
Theft Auto. Word went around the Internet like wildfire that by
pushing certain keys during certain chase scenes, players could view
explicitly lewd sexual material. Until the information was with-
drawn, sales of the video mushroomed. Of course, parents were the
last to hear about this abomination. No one knows how many other
games may be relying on such means to boost sales.

An expert in the field of video games and author of A Theory of
Fun for Game Designers (2005), Ralph Koster has a singularly negative view of his colleagues' work: "Games thus far . . . have been an
arena where human behavior—often in its crudest, most primitive
form—is put on display. . . . Right now, most games are about violence. They are about power. They are about control. . . . We should
fix the fact that the average cartoon does a better job of portraying
the human condition than our games do" (pp. 175–176).

It must be conceded that the overall verdict is not in. Studies
have disagreed over whether violent video games and media exposure have violent effects on some children. The most important de-
fense you can have, therefore, is to know your child. Children who
have difficulty discriminating between fantasy and reality may be
more susceptible to becoming violent. They also may be highly sen-

sitive to visual images and may express themselves more intensely than their peers. Another possibility is that some children pick violent video games because they have a predisposition toward violent behavior. Something else may have caused a disturbance emotionally in a child that causes a preference for violent video games and television. Thus, their playing the games may be the result rather than the cause of their personality.

What to Do About Video Games

- Become involved in your children's video game choices. Simply scanning the packaging advertising is not sufficient.

- In order to avoid negative effects of video games, you should try playing them yourself.

- Talk to your kids about what they play when they're at someone else's house, and listen to hear what games they talk about with their friends. Ask them questions about why they like the games they play, how they feel when they play, and what they think tends to happen when they stop playing a game.

- It is important to monitor each video game's rating. The Entertainment Software Ratings Board's Web site explains the ratings for parents: http://www.childdevelopmentinfo.com/ health_safety/video_game_rating_system.htm.

Pornography and the Media

Children, especially boys ages twelve to seventeen, find it easy to get pornography. They can obtain it on most media: television, the Internet, magazines, books, phone hot lines, and videos. The amount of pornographic material available to boys has increased because of the variety of media sources that can make money on it.

In previous generations, it was not uncommon for young boys to view pornographic material from time to time, but only a few of them owned their own material. Sometimes they would look at their parents' magazines, but they were seldom able to purchase them on their own. Today those barriers do not exist. For example, children can easily access everything that they want from their computers without their parents even knowing it. Furthermore, pornography now is much different from what it was years ago. It now includes much harsher images, including sadomasochism, violence, and sexual assault.

One main problem with excessive pornographic viewing is that it influences the values of the viewers. Pornography often teaches viewers to objectify women, who are the subjects of rough violence and sadomasochism. Boys may get the idea that women want to be taken advantage of, taken sexually by force, or be raped. Pornography frequently depicts sex as an act completely separate from love or respect. Such values may affect your child's sex life later on.

Perhaps the biggest concern of pornographic viewing is that it teaches detachment of sex from any sort of responsibility. As a result, children may be enticed to engage in sexual activity without considering the possible negative effects of unplanned pregnancy, sexually transmitted diseases, and greater tolerance toward rape. One study showed that male viewers are more likely to feel as though women are responsible for being raped and should not resist.

Some media, especially sexual hot lines, cause an addictive attitude toward sex. It has been found to be as addictive and dangerous as gambling and may even create a chemical dependency not unlike that of alcohol or drugs. There are very few restrictions on access to pornographic hot lines. Even when a parent places restrictions on calls from the home, children often find phones in other places from which to make the calls. Some restrictions have been placed on these phone sex companies; however, they seem to find ways around them. In one study of pornographic phone calls, every participant wanted to go back to make more calls. This included boys and girls, preteens and teens.

About 60 percent of males and 40 percent of females exposed to hard-core porn expressed a desire to try to mimic the behavior that they just witnessed. In addition, almost one-third of males and

18 percent of females in high school admitted to partaking in a sexual act that they viewed in pornography. These acts took place within a few days of the viewing.

Pornography often takes the place of sexual education. This is especially unfortunate, because sexual education uses pictures and diagrams of sexual information that is carefully chosen and does not degrade women or include minors or encourage violent sexual acts.

CHANTAL'S DISAPPOINTING DISCOVERY

Skimming through the pages of *Family Circle* magazine one day, Chantal found another of those articles she loves. Her favorites are the ones that offer lots of information about how to run her home better, ideas she would never think of herself. This one had to do with bedrooms. Tucked in between recommendations for killing dust mites and dusting blinds was a tip about mattresses.

"Even if the mattresses your family sleeps on are of the best, most expensive quality," it stated, "the materials that keep those mattresses from sagging will weaken with time and use. You can prolong a mattress's life and functionality by turning it often. It isn't always easy to do, but it's worth it in terms of money saved and many more good nights' sleep!"

Chantal knew she would have to wait until Jack came home to turn their own mattress, but she could do the ones in her kids' rooms herself. Both of them sleep on a twin-sized bed so the job would be easy. She decided to flip them and leave them unmade for the day to give them a good airing out.

She started in the bedroom of her fifteen-year-old son, Lewan. After stripping the bed as she usually does, she lifted the mattress and stood it on its side. At first she was so surprised to find anything under there that she blinked. Near the center of the box springs were three glossy magazines and two videotapes. Pushing the mattress off the side of the bed, she picked up one of the magazines. Her hearted started to pound. She knew such publications existed and had once asked Jack if he had any interest in looking at them. "Only the articles," he had joked.

But her son? How did he know about them? Where did he get them? Why did he have them? After flipping through the first couple of pages, she felt she was going to be sick. They were much more explicit than she had ever imagined. She was horrified to think that these pictures were teaching her child that this was what sex was like. Oral, anal, two women with each other: it went against everything she believed in. "Oh, this can't possibly be Lewan's."

The photos were bad enough, but when she inserted the tape into the player in the family room, she really thought she would vomit. She had assumed she would see some kind of introductory images, but the tape had been stopped in the middle. The screen was filled with images that were not only obscene to her but unimaginable, completely vile. Swiftly she yanked out the tape and shut off the player and TV.

Then it struck her: some disgusting person had sold these offensive items to her teenaged boy. As a result, Lewan's head was filled with sickening ideas of what normal people do. He was violated just as surely as if he had been sexually abused. True, the damage wouldn't be as great as if a person had actually raped him, but Lewan's soul was befouled. Her nausea turned to rage. "Wait until Jack gets home," she thought. "We'll find this person and make him pay for his crime!"

She couldn't wait. She called Jack at work, needing to vent her fury immediately. When she had described what she had found, she asked, "Do you think we should call the police or the principal? Would that get Lewan in trouble? What are we going to do with him anyway?" To her dismay, Jack did not react as she expected. "Now, wait a minute," he replied. "I think you're overreacting. It's nothing he wouldn't see on the Internet. Besides, it may be a good way for him to learn about sexuality. There was a lot I didn't know about sex that I should have, and I don't want Lewan to be as ignorant as I was. Let's just pretend nothing happened."

"I just can't live with that, Jack," she explained. "It's just plain wrong."

"Okay, Chantal, if that is how you feel about it, but you're going to have to be the one to talk with him."

"I suppose it is fair, since I am the one with the problem, so I'll talk with him. But how am I going to even mention those nasty sex scenes to him?" Chantal thinks to herself for a moment and decides to call her best friend, Jan, as she always does, to see what she thinks.

On the phone, Chantal explains her situation. Jan has several more years as a mother, and her boys are several years older than Chantal's son. When Chantal explains the whole situation to her, Jan exclaims, "Oh, I know exactly what you are talking about."

"You do?"

"Oh, I have been through this with each of my boys. I think I can tell you from experience that this is going to require that you do some homework first. Before you can talk to Lewan, you are going to have to become much more comfortable with this subject yourself. Otherwise he will sense that you don't know what you are talking about and won't listen to a word you say."

Jan first explains to Chantal that she should start with diagrams and pictures of both the female and male reproductive organs. She recommends that Chantal go to the bookstore and buy an adult psychology text, and in this book there will be a chapter on physical development that she will need. Alternatively, she can look for these pictures on the Internet. Chantal is not that familiar with the Internet, so she takes Jan's advice and buys a used copy of a textbook. She looks up the diagrams of the male and female sexual organs in a book and reports to Jan that she had no idea how complex these systems are. Jan suggests that it is not enough simply to look at the pictures. She must continue to study them until she no longer becomes squeamish. After spending the afternoon becoming knowledgeable about these drawings, Chantal calls Jan and says, "I don't like doing this much, but I am more comfortable with them now. I guess I am ready to move on. What's next?"

Jan urges her to go to the video store and rent some movies that show couples acting in a sexy way. She recommends that Chantal rent *Pretty Woman* and *The Mirror Has Two Faces* and watch the sexual scenes over and over again until she feels comfortable. After viewing the videos multiple times, she writes down what each of the movies is about, then recites what she wrote in front of the mirror. At first, Chantal has a difficult time enunciating particular sexual words out loud in front of the mirror. Eventually she begins to relax and is able for the first time to talk to her husband about their sex life.

Chantal calls Jan once more and states that although she has made a lot of progress, she still has no idea how she is going to confront her son about the explicit sexual material. Jan tells Chantal that she should write down what she wants to say and practice, as she did with the movies. Chantal sits at her computer and starts to write down everything she wants to say to her son. After she finishes writing, she reads her speech in front of the mirror and then she reads it to her husband. Finally, she and Jan role-play the discussion over the phone.

Although she is a bit nervous, Chantal is able to talk to Lewan when he comes home from school the next afternoon about the materials that she found in his room. She is relieved to find that his reaction was to ask her about sexual practices, and, thanks to Jan's and her husband's help, she is able to answer them. She and her son found that they felt closer to each other as a result of the experience.

What to Do About Pornography

- The most important way to prevent your children from learning about sex through pornography is to talk to them directly. Unless they can be persuaded to stay away from it, they will get it, one way or another.

- We recommend that the father or other trusted male talk to sons first. Advice coming from a man who can explain why it is important to treat women with respect and not as objects is most likely to be effective. When a boy hears from his father that sex should be about love and respect, mutual respect between both parties, and not about male domination of women, it will enforce values opposite those portrayed in pornography.

- Use the techniques for controlling your children's access to the Internet described in this chapter. Try to find out if your child is gaining access to pornographic materials in the homes of friends. Ask around, and use whatever sources you can to get this information.

- Be on the alert for sexual obsessions in your children. If you find that after carrying out the advice in the preceding paragraphs, you suspect your child is manifesting an addiction to pornography, you need to seek the help of a counselor.

Webcams: A New Pornography Problem

Perhaps the scariest innovation on the Internet, in the hands of young teens at least, is the Web camera (called a Webcam). This eyeball-shaped camera can be attached to the lid of a laptop computer or set on a stand. With an inexpensive Webcam (it costs about twenty-five dollars) and free software, teens can transmit live voice videos of themselves. Typically teens use Webcams to see the friend they are talking to and to be seen by that friend. Unfortunately, because the Internet is accessible to anyone, child molesters can also view these sessions. The teen announces that he is online, and pornographic abusers respond, pretending to be another teen who wants to be friends.

It all starts innocently enough, with the molester bestowing complements on the vulnerable teen, especially about how good-looking he is. Often youth with the lowest self-esteem are the most attracted to this medium, because they lack an adequate social network in their lives. In the case of one such teen, Justin Berry, a thirteen-year-old Californian, his correspondent simply asked him to remove his shirt and offered him fifty dollars for doing so. Justin received the reward through PayPal, an online financial exchange service that his new friend set up for him. Reasoning that he regularly took his shirt off in public in the summertime, Justin complied. "Easy money," he thought.

Over the next five years, completely unknown to his otherwise attentive parents, Justin was seduced into doing nude sexual poses, masturbating, and having intercourse, all in front of the camera. The audience watching his shows grew, at the invitation of the original abuser. Before he quit, he was being watched by as many as fifteen hundred viewers and was paid hundreds of thousands of dollars for his actions, which he carefully saved to avoid being discovered. His sponsor even rented an apartment for him near his home, so that he could perform while allegedly playing with friends. Justin now helps authorities catch those who make a practice of seducing young Webcam users. Nevertheless, videos of his sessions were recorded digitally and are still available on the Net. Justin's notoriety is unlikely to fade in the immediate future. "This has screwed me up big time," he laments.

We would like to think that Justin's case is unique, but teen use of Webcams for illicit purposes has been growing at an exponential rate according to authorities. It isn't limited to males either. Females have discovered that movies of themselves posturing in sexy clothing can attract interest. This behavior also can put them at risk of becoming prey to the molesters who spend hours scouring the Net for teen Web sites. The most effective way to protect your children from these results is to monitor their use of the Webcam or forbid its use altogether.

Music

Music has long been an integral media source in the life of teenagers. Researchers find that teens spend as much as five hours a day listening to music. The most common music that many listen to today is rap. There is a growing concern about the values and attitudes that are portrayed in these songs. According to the American Academy of Child and Adolescent Psychiatry, this type of music has troublesome aspects in that it

- Advocates the use of drugs, cigarettes, and alcohol as cool and attractive, not unhealthy and deadly
- Suggests that fighting and other violent acts should be used as a way to handle conflict
- Describes antiauthority attitudes, such as "offing the cops"
- Argues that suicide can be a valid solution to an unhappy life
- Promotes harmful and unsafe graphic sexual practices
- Devalues women, often violently

In a recent survey, 47 percent of mothers with children in public schools believe that violent messages in rap music contribute to the increase in school violence. However, experts differ as to the overall effects of rap music on America's youth. Although many studies have demonstrated a correlation between the media and the behavior of children and teens, some agree with UCLA professor of ethnomusicology Cheryl Keyes, who points out that in addition to considering exposure to rap, we also need to look at the effect of parenting on the children. Another view is that of researcher Ralph DiClemente of Emory University. He believes that rap music mainly affects vulnerable social groups. DiClemente studied fourteen- to eighteen-year-old, nonurban, sexually active black girls in Birmingham, Alabama. He found that those who watched rap videos for fourteen or more hours each week were more likely to hit a teacher, have multiple sexual partners, get arrested, drink, use drugs, and get sexually transmitted diseases.

Teen music television, mainly the cable channels MTV and VH1, has redefined music with the creation of music videos, which are widely viewed by teenagers. Music videos, which also sell separately, bring together rock music with visual images, which have also caused a great deal of concern among adults. In a presentation in 2004, researcher Bronwyn Mayden focused on the negative elements of the videos, including a degrading presentation of women, the portrayal of sexuality aimed at twelve- to nineteen-year-old viewers, and failure to portray the negative consequences of early sexuality. Mayden urged pressure on Congress to limit exposure to children as a way to minimize the negative effects of these videos.

What to Do About Music

- Be aware of the type of music your children are listening to. Pay attention to the lyrics of the songs, and if you hear inappropriate language or attitudes, discuss the ramifications with your children.

- Make clear the types of music that are acceptable and exactly why some is unacceptable.

- Find out what types of music your children like. There may be some music that is inoffensive to you but that they should not be allowed to take to school because it will offend others.

- Music can be a great way to connect with your children. Expose them to a wide variety of music, such as taking them to concerts and listening to radio stations that broadcast inoffensive music that appeals to children and teens.

- Explain the art of music to your children, and help them to see the way music can have a positive impact on their lives.
- Watch for signs of the bad effects of too much listening to this music:

     Poor school performance

     Frequent hitting or pushing of other kids

     Aggressive talking back to adults

     Frequent nightmares

     Increased eating of unhealthy foods

     Smoking, drinking, or drug use

The bottom line is that, like pornographic sex and violence portrayed on other media, rap and music videos are unlikely to have a good impact on your children's values and may well have a negative effect. If you can find a way to keep your children from listening to and watching such negative behaviors, you probably should.

In the final analysis, the only real safeguard is to look at or listen to the media described in this chapter with your children and discuss what they think. Get them to tell you their honest opinions of the material, listen carefully to what they have to say (see Chapter Eleven for advice on how to do this), and avoid telling them what they should think. Your best chance for them to adapt reasonable attitudes is that as they explain their attitudes, they are better able to think clearly and to live the values you have taught them.

6

DRUG AND ALCOHOL ABUSE

"Do You Want to Wind Up in the Gutter?"

When it comes to the abuse of drugs and alcohol, there is good news—and there is bad news too.

THE BAD NEWS

Alcohol

Researchers believe that over 90 percent of high school students have tried alcohol at some time in their lives. How much do they drink? It's hard to tell for sure. Studies use different definitions of *misuse*, and as a result they produce widely different estimates. One finding is clear: too many school-aged children drink excessively too often. Here are our best estimates:

- Over the past year, high school boys engaged in at least one high-risk drinking activity at the same rate as girls: about two-thirds. Whites and Hispanics have higher levels of misuse than Asians, and African Americans drink the least.

- Adolescents who begin drinking before age fifteen are four times more likely to develop alcohol dependence than those who begin drinking at age twenty-one.

- Teens who smoke cigarettes are more likely to try alcohol.

- One-third of teens in a large study view drinking four or five alcoholic drinks nearly every day as no great risk to health. Fully one-half feel that drinking four or five alcoholic drinks once or twice a week is safe.

- More than a quarter of all alcohol consumed in the United States is drunk by people under the age of twenty.

- Of those youth who are ages twelve to seventeen and who drank any alcohol in the past year, 39 percent had at least one serious problem as a result of alcohol in the past year, and 18 percent developed tolerance to the effects of alcohol.

- It has been estimated that over 3 million teenagers are alcoholics. Several million more have a serious drinking problem that they cannot manage on their own.

Marijuana

There is debate about whether marijuana smoking is as dangerous as drinking. Because it is hard to determine what would be an equal amount of the two substances, there are no reliable comparison studies. It is clear, however, that regular use can lead to deleterious effects, such as lung cancer and gynecomastia (swollen breasts in males). In addition:

- Teens who smoke tobacco and drink alcohol are more likely to try marijuana.

- The use of marijuana often leads to the use of other illicit drugs.

- One out of every five eighth graders has tried marijuana.

- Thirty-six percent of parents believe their teen perceives trying marijuana once or twice as taking a great risk. Only 19 percent of teens actually agree.

- Seventeen percent of parents believe their teen has marijuana-using friends, but 62 percent of teens say they have friends who use marijuana.

- Eighteen percent of parents say that their teen has tried marijuana, but 39 percent of teens say they have.

- Fifty percent of kids will try marijuana before they graduate high school.

Designer Drugs

Designer drugs (such as speed, methamphetamine, and uppers) are new drugs created by making a minor modification in the chemical structure of an existing drug. The result is a new substance with pharmacological effects similar to those of the original substance. Early designer drugs were created as substitutes for heroin, amphetamines, and hallucinogens. Ecstasy is one of the more publicized designer drugs, or "club drugs."

Many designer drugs are easy to make, and the "labs" can be built and kept in an area as simple as a kitchen sink. The relatively cheap prices and easy availability on the street can mean real trouble for users, since dangers are related to how the drugs are made as well as how they're used.

One of the main features that teens find appealing about designer drugs is the almost instant, intense rush achieved by snorting or smoking the substance. These stimulants affect the central nervous system, which means that teens put themselves at risk for brain damage and paralysis every time they use the drugs. In addition:

- Almost 27 percent of high school seniors reported that they could easily access "crystal meth," the smokable "rock" form of methamphetamine.

- According to government statistics (www.dea.gov), emergency room mentions for methamphetamine increased by almost 20 percent between 2000 and 2002, and emergency room mentions for oxycodone nearly tripled.

- Designer drug use increases energy and reduces appetite. Repeated use creates a tolerance that leads many teens to use more of these drugs more often.

Inhalants

Teenagers' abuse of inhalants is on the rise. Common inhalants are hair spray, glue, shoe polish, furniture spray, paint thinners, and cleaning fluids. Health and social effects of inhalants are brain and neural damage, convulsions, deafness, impaired vision, depressed motor skills, behavioral problems, and other drug use and delinquent behavior. In 2003, more than 2 million people reported using inhalants, and 1.1 million of those were aged twelve to seventeen. Awareness of the dangers of inhalants is low among teenagers, and fewer parents are discussing these dangers with their children. If you have any suspicions that one of your children is interested in experimenting with inhalants, you must make these substances unavailable. Make sure all of your children are aware of the dangerous and life-threatening consequences of inhalant use.

THE GOOD NEWS

The good news is very important:

- Children who learn about the dangers of drugs and alcohol from their parents are 42 percent less likely to use those substances and more likely to avoid other risky behaviors.
- Two-thirds of kids who do not smoke marijuana or use other drugs say they refrain out of fear of losing their parents' respect.

ACTIONS TO TAKE AGAINST ABUSE OF DRUGS AND ALCOHOL

Because of the nature of addiction, we do this section a bit differently from the other chapters. That is because what you do to handle this threat will likely depend on the cause of the problem. We look here at the reasons that kids turn to alcohol or drugs and what to do about each problem.

Boredom

Many kids today have a lot of unsupervised free time, especially if both of their parents work full time, and they lack constructive ways to use it.

Actions to Take

- Encourage involvement in after-school activities. Become knowledgeable about programs offered at school and in the community, such as athletics, the arts, and youth groups.

- Suggest simple activities to occupy time, such as reading or hiking.

- Foster creative attitudes in your children so they will be more likely to think of engaging pastimes (see Chapter Five.)

- When appropriate, encourage your teen to get a job or volunteer during the summer or on weekends.

Vulnerability to Advertising

When it comes to alcohol advertising, few marketers demonstrate reluctance to mislead vulnerable teens. In fact, there is a set of myths that they often try to promulgate:

1. Everyone drinks alcohol.

2. Drinking has no risks.

3. Drinking helps to solve problems.

4. Alcohol is a magic potion that can transform you.

5. Sports and alcohol go together.

6. If alcohol were truly dangerous, we wouldn't be advertising it.

7. Alcoholic beverage companies only promote drinking in moderation.

In fact, these same myths are promoted by drug dealers and other teens to push substance abuse. Doubtless you can readily see how phony each of the "arguments" is. Your children, who may well want to try using alcohol or drugs, may either not see how false they are or, more likely, will succeed in rationalizing them away. Nothing exposes these myths like open discussion. Just getting your teens to talk about them in a straightforward manner will usually explode them. There are other ways you can combat these myths.

Actions to Take

- Numerous Web sites deal with the truth about these allegations (see the Appendix). Visit them with your child.
- Ask whether your school system has invited recovering alcoholics or abusers to talk to students specifically about these myths.
- Ask your teen to write an article about these myths, and provide assistance in getting the article published in the school newspaper.

To Have a Good Time and Feel Good

Alcohol and drugs lower inhibitions and allow teens to open up and feel they are having fun in social settings.

Actions to Take

- Set an example for your teen. Demonstrate that you can have fun and still be accepted in a social setting without the use of substances.
- Support their involvement with school and community activities that foster structured social time.

- Teach your children to respect themselves physically, mentally, emotionally, and spiritually.

To Fit In and Be Cool

When friends are experimenting with alcohol and drugs, peer pressure proves a powerful influence. No one, especially a teen, wants to be an outcast.

Actions to Take

- Tell your children they can use their parents as an excuse: "My mom would kill me if she thought I smoked pot."
- Be sensitive to the effects of peer pressure, and make sure you understand your children's concerns.
- Offer stories from your own experience or advice on how to deal with peer pressure.
- Encourage independent thinking. This will help prevent the "everyone does it" excuse.

Curiosity

Alcohol and drugs appear mysterious and exciting.

Actions to Take

- Explain the concrete and real effects of substance use to show that the costs outweigh the benefits.
- Encourage healthy curiosity in well-supervised settings (see the story about Denise on page 91).

Rebellion

The teen years are naturally a time of exploration and rebellion against established rules and value systems.

Actions to Take

- Discipline rebellion, and explain to your child the reason for the punishment so that he or she understands the reasoning behind your actions.
- Allow your children to explore their individuality by encouraging dialogue, such as discussing their differing viewpoints.

Escape from Reality

Teens deal with enormous amounts of stress, especially as they try to discover themselves and fit in. Alcohol and drugs become a way to escape.

Actions to Take

- Set an example. Never refer to an alcoholic beverage as a way to escape. In other words, do not say: "Man, I've had a rough day! I really need a drink."
- Allow your children time to communicate their anxieties. Be understanding of the fact that this may mean they need time alone.
- Offer healthy alternatives to escaping, such as meditation and reflection.

Low Self-Esteem

At different ages, children compare their abilities to those of others, such as friends and family. Teens are especially susceptible to negative self-esteem as peers' opinions take on heightened importance.

Actions to Take

- Make sure your children clearly understand how much you love them unconditionally. Compliment them; talk to them about their good qualities and strengths.

- Encourage strong friendships to support the development of self-worth.
- Encourage them to pursue passions and talents so they can experience validation and support from outside sources.

Lack of Knowledge and Communication

Children often assume that they know all the facts without considering the consequences of their actions. They perceive they are invincible and don't need to seek advice or permission from adults.

Actions to Take

- Be informed about drugs and alcohol. Teach your children how to avoid substances, and fully explain the consequences of using them. Just "trying it" is not okay.
- Turn ordinary moments into teachable moments. If you see teenagers smoking in the park, talk to your child about smoking. When kids observe the behavior, they will understand and connect ideas more easily.
- Discover available resources at school and in the community. Inquire about how drug and alcohol awareness is taught to your children so you can work with the school.
- Telling your children, "This medicine will make your head feel better but too much will give you a stomachache" conveys the idea that the same substance can be both good and bad.
- The key is not to preach or lecture. Have discussions with your kids about drugs, and use open-ended questions. Show that you are open and willing to discuss the issues. Current events provide great opportunities to talk to your kids, especially popular issues that receive a lot of media attention, such as the use of steroids in sports.
- Be aware of the influence of the media and technology on your children. The Internet has easily accessible sites about

drugs and paraphernalia. Dealers and suppliers can meet in chatrooms and arrange deliveries.

No Clear Set of Rules Established by Parents

Teens often say that no one told them they couldn't use a specific drug or drink a particular drink. This is obviously rationalizing, but there are some effective ways to avoid it.

Actions to Take

- When there are two parents in a household, make sure you discuss the rules beforehand and work together to enforce them.
- Discuss with your teen the boundaries you set and why you set them so he or she knows the rules and understands the reasons and values behind the rules.
- Ask your teen for his or her input, making it clear, however, that your word is final. Make your opinion on drugs and alcohol very clear.
- Set a curfew, and have your children say goodnight to you when they are back home.
- Make it easy for your kids to come home. Explain that you will pick them up under any circumstances, no questions asked.

Inconsistent Parental Rules

As you undoubtedly know from being a teenager yourself, playing one parent off against the other is a favorite technique. You and your partner must stand together when it comes to substance abuse.

Actions to Take

- Start an ongoing discussion about drugs and alcohol. Ask your children if they have tried alcohol or drugs and if these substances are present at parties. Make sure they know what is expected of them at social events.

- Use techniques in this book to create greater family cohesiveness, as the teen years are a time of separation from parental influence. See *The Joyful Family* (Dacey and Weygint, 2002) for additional information.

- Create a network of communication with the parents of your teen's friends. Get to know your teen's friends.

- Know where you're teen is going, and stay connected through phone calls.

- If your teen is going to a party, call the parents of the teenage host to see if they will be home during the party.

- Keep lines of communication open by inquiring about your teen's activities. Have a family calendar to keep track of everyone's schedules.

- Don't go too far! Do not invade your children's privacy by having breathalyzers or refusing to allow time with friends. You must set reasonable boundaries and follow up on them.

WARNING SIGNS OF DRUG OR ALCOHOL ABUSE

Teenagers who are developing serious alcohol or drug problems usually exhibit similar symptoms:

- Depression for more than two weeks
- Rapid drop in self-esteem
- Repeated health complaints
- Red, puffy, or glazed eyes
- Withdrawing from family activities
- Repeated truancy
- Problems with the law

- Changes to less conventional styles in dress and music
- Falling grades
- Feelings of not fitting in
- Neglect of hygiene and appearance
- Rapid weight gain or loss
- Sneaky behavior and increased secrecy
- Lack of enthusiasm about things that they used to value
- Lying even when there is no reason to lie
- Reckless behavior and increased rule breaking
- Missing money or valuables
- Possession of drug paraphernalia

Of course, other factors could cause any one of these signs. If, however, you notice several of them at a time, you should investigate. Spying on your child, such as going through her things or asking questions of his friends, is usually not advisable. Under these circumstances, however, it may well be necessary in order to protect her from the dire consequences of substance abuse. Should you find out your child is abusing alcohol or drugs, do not panic. Do not blame yourself, even if you have a family history of substance abuse. Confront your child when he or she is able to have a conversation and allow him or her time to speak. If necessary, seek professional help.

DENISE'S MOM USED DRUGS WHEN SHE WAS A TEEN— WHY SHOULDN'T DENISE?

Denise Ouimet's mother, Sophie, knew it was time to talk to her twelve-year-old daughter about using drugs and alcohol, but she has dreaded the conversation. She felt like a hypocrite, telling Denise to stay away from the stuff because when Sophie was in high school, she didn't. Although she didn't drink a lot, she did get drunk a few times, and she smoked marijuana at least once a week during the second half of her senior year.

Finally, Sophie decided to go to her sixty-seven-year-old aunt, Joanne, who is known in the family for her sage advice.

What she heard from her aunt helped. "First of all," Joanne told her, "those were different times. There was an atmosphere of experimentation—with politics, sex, family relations, as well as with drugs. Several famous psychiatrists believed that psychogenic drugs were good for us! We didn't know just how harmful those substances could be. There's a lot more research now indicating that even occasional use of beer, wine coolers, and marijuana can be dangerous for people who have a genetic predisposition to addiction to these substances. Also, higher-risk drugs like cocaine, Ecstasy, and inhalants were used much less frequently back then. The penalties for use were much less stringent. You were just plain lucky, and most of us had enough sense to stop in time. You need to get over yourself and talk to your daughter before another day goes by!"

The next day, Joanne called Sophie saying, "Your Uncle Dennis and I have been talking, and we think we have an idea that might help you with Denise. Tell her that if she can swear that she has never tried drugs when she graduates from high school, we will give her money for new clothes for college. We asked my brother and my two sisters to donate, and between us we can offer her $1,950, which she'll get only if she keeps the deal."

When Sophie talked to Denise about using drugs, the subject of Sophie's own use never came up. Denise was so happy about the financial offer that apparently her mother's past experience never crossed her mind, and she readily agreed.

Six months later, Denise did say that she was curious about Sophie's drug use when she was a teen. Sophie didn't lie to her, but used the arguments that Joanne had given her. Then she said, "But that doesn't excuse it, Denise. I knew it was wrong and dangerous. In fact, I could tell I was starting to need the drug somewhat, and that scared me. I've never done it again, and I consider myself very lucky. I don't know if I have the addiction gene or not, but I don't want to find out. I hope you don't either." To Sophie's surprise, Denise found her statements quite reasonable and promised to continue toward her goal of winning the money from her uncles and aunts. "Even if I weren't getting money for it," Denise told her, "I think your advice is good. But I must admit, that prize is helping me stay motivated to keep my word!"

At her graduation party, Denise was able to take an oath that she had complied with the terms of the deal, and in truth, she had. Of even greater benefit to her, she had gotten valuable practice resisting peer pressure and refusing offers of marijuana and alcohol. This experience helped Denise many times in college. As a result, she made it through the four years with almost no regrets, none of which included substance abuse.

If we could determine the true costs of youthful substance abuse to our society as a whole, not just in terms of money but also in mental disturbance, other illnesses, and deaths, we would probably be astounded. The biggest problem is our own complacency. A parent was seen walking into his son's college dormitory on a football home game Saturday with a case of wine on his shoulder and a case of beer under his arm. He was asked why he was doing it. "Oh, lighten up," he said. "Didn't you drink in college?" He won't think it's dangerous until something awful happens to his son.

It's unclear when society will take a more mature position on this problem. But you can start today.

7

CHILD ABUSE

"Whom Can You Trust These Days?"

In the first part of this chapter, we will deal with the common view of abuse—that is, of children by adults. However, mothers have made it clear that they are also concerned about date abuse. Later in the chapter we look at the latest information in this arena as well.

Classifications of child abuse used in the media have led to some confusion. We offer the following definitions, on which most professionals agree:

- *Neglect* is failure to provide for a child's basic needs. Neglect may be physical, medical, educational, or emotional. Sometimes cultural values, the standards of care in the community, and poverty may be contributing factors, indicating the family is in need of information or assistance. When a family fails to use information and resources and the child's health or safety is at risk, child welfare intervention may be required.
- *Physical abuse* is physical injury (ranging from minor bruises to severe fractures or death) as a result of punching, beating, kicking, biting, shaking, throwing, stabbing, choking, hitting (with a hand, stick, strap, or other object), burning, or otherwise harming a child. Such injury is considered abuse regardless of whether the caretaker intended to hurt the child.
- *Sexual abuse* includes activities by a parent or caretaker such as fondling a child's genitals, penetration, incest, rape, sodomy, in-

decent exposure, and exploitation through prostitution or the production of pornographic materials.

- *Emotional abuse* is a pattern of behavior that impairs a child's emotional development or sense of self-worth. It almost always accompanies the other types of abuse.

SOME FACTS ABOUT THE PREVALENCE OF ABUSE

Sexual abuse of children is a tragic problem affecting children of all ages and from all walks of life. It is not widespread, but it happens often enough to be a cause for great concern. Some children are abused by strangers, but that is rare. More often they are abused by someone they know and trust: a relative, friend, neighbor, coach, baby-sitter, scout leader, parent, or cleric. Sexual abuse is not usually a violent act. The child is involved in "games" or seduction over a period of time.

Nearly 900,000 children were determined to be victims of child abuse or neglect in 2002, according to a large national study. This amounts to a rate of 12 children per 1,000. That figure has dropped from 13.4 children in 1990. About 60 percent of child victims were neglected by their parents or other caregivers. Nearly 20 percent suffered physical abuse, 10 percent were sexually abused, and the rest were emotionally maltreated.

We can't be certain of these figures because child abuse is also a secret problem: children often do not tell anyone that someone has hurt them. Sometimes they don't say anything because they don't want to upset their parents or they are embarrassed. Children often think, and are told, that what is happening is their own fault. Or they may believe that no one cares what happens to them. They might be frightened by the abuser's threats to harm family members if the child tells "the secret." Young children may not even know there is something to tell; they are taught to respect and obey adults. The number of children in child care is steadily increasing. The American Psychological Association feels that family child care must be included in the national strategy for the prevention and treatment of child abuse and neglect. Child care programs can help reduce child abuse in a variety of ways. These include providing supports to high-risk families and training child care staff in appropriate child behavior management strategies and procedures for detecting and reporting child abuse.

FAMILY CHARACTERISTICS THAT CAN LEAD TO ABUSE

Many studies have shown that certain family characteristics may contribute to child abuse. One major characteristic is family stress: child care problems, financial problems, and maternal depression, for example. Families with multiple stressors tend to have more domestic violence and child maltreatment. Studies have also shown that high-risk families are more socially isolated. Families that do not receive support from social services, religious organizations, or other social networks find themselves at a greater risk for problems, mainly child abuse. A third major characteristic of families that has shown to correlate to child abuse is poor parenting skills. Parents who mistreat their children lack certain parenting skills. These are parents who rarely monitor their children's activities, rarely supervise their children, and have less positive interaction with their children.

ACTIONS TO TAKE TO DEAL WITH CHILD ABUSE

Fortunately, there are many ways you and your family can keep your children safe from abuse.

What You Can Do to Deal with Abuse

- Listen carefully for clues. The one most reliable sign of sexual abuse is that the child says this is happening, but it may be in a roundabout way, for example, "I really don't want to go to Uncle Ray's house right now."

- Take your child for a medical exam if you see any of the following signs: venereal disease, as indicated by vaginal or penile discharge or irritated or itching genitals or anus (children cannot catch venereal disease from nonsexual means); pregnancy; pain or injury to areas of the genitals or the mouth; urinary difficulty; or unusual cuts and bruises.

- Often there are no physical signs when a child has been sexually abused. Behavior changes are more common. Here are some behavioral changes to look for:

    Fear of a person or certain places, such as showers and washrooms

    Reverting to babyish habits like thumb sucking

    Interest in own or others' genitals, sexual acts, and sexual words

    Sexual behavior that is inappropriate for the child's age

    Acting-out sexual or abusive behavior with toys, animals, or other children (this is an especially important sign)

    Nightmares, bedwetting, fear of the dark, difficulty falling asleep, other new fears

    Overreaction when the child is questioned about being touched

- Be careful not to plant ideas in your child's mind. Repeatedly asking questions about abuse can do that. Ask open-ended questions, for example, "I sense that something's not okay with you. What are you thinking about?"

- Make sure that if what you are hearing upsets you, you don't show it.

- If your child does tell you about being sexually abused, accept what your child says as the truth. Don't deny or ignore it. If in doubt, err on the child's side.

- Protect your child immediately from the suspected offender. You can start repairing the damage at once by assuring your child that the abuse will not continue. Assure your child that it is not his or her fault, that you are glad he or she told, and that there are many people who will help your family.

- Don't promise anything that you can't control. For example, don't promise that the offender will go to jail.

- Report the abuse to the authorities immediately. If the abuse was by a member of your household or in a foster home or day care setting, call the Child Abuse and Maltreatment hot line at 1-800-342-3720.

- If the abuse was by someone else outside your family, report it to the local or state police or sheriff's department.

- When the authorities interview your child about suspected child abuse, stay with and reassure him or her. A specialist trained in child sexual abuse should do the interviewing.

- Find support for yourself. Take care of your own feelings, for your child's sake as well as your own.

- Try to keep your household activities as normal as possible.

- Take your child to see a counselor who specializes in child sexual abuse.

What to Say to Your Children About Abuse of Any Kind

"Has a grown-up or another child ever said or done anything that hurt or made you feel uncomfortable?"

"Abusing children, or anyone else, is wrong. And it's never the fault of the person being abused."

"Many children have felt a bad touch at some time in their lives. Bad touches, like hitting, pinching, or kicking, hurt and are no fun. When touch feels bad or confusing, it can also be abuse, especially when you ask someone to stop, and they don't."

"Your body belongs only to you. This is especially true for the parts that are covered by your bathing suit: breasts, vagina, and bottom for girls and penis and bottom for boys. If someone other than your mommy or daddy or a medical person touches your private parts or tells you to touch them, it is sexual abuse. If that happens, I want you to tell me. Of course, when really little children need help with their baths or need their diapers changed, that isn't sexual abuse."

"There are other types of abuse that can happen without touching. If someone yells all the time, makes threats, calls names, and never hugs a child, this can be verbal or emotional abuse."

"It's important to remember that most people are harmless and won't abuse you, but unfortunately, there are some people who do abuse. If you even suspect that someone is abusing you, I want you to come and tell me right away."

IF YOU ARE TEMPTED TO HURT YOUR CHILD

Many parents do not know how to punish their children without spanking them. But there have been studies indicating negative effects on a child who is spanked: low self-esteem, depression, bullying, and accepting lower-paid jobs. So instead of spanking your child, here are some alternatives:

- Give appropriate consequences for bad behavior; make the consequence fit the action. If children steal, they have to make remuneration for the theft. Show your children how they can make amends.
- Speak calmly and firmly, with direct eye contact.
- Stay calm, or leave the situation temporarily if you have to.

- If your child throws a tantrum, do nothing until the tantrum has run its course. Instructing the child to stop acting that way will only reinforce the tantrum.

- If the situation has made you very angry, let your anger out in a way that will not hurt anyone. For example, pound on a pillow until you feel better.

- Call someone who is sympathetic to talk about your frustrations and who will give you suggestions on how to handle the situation safely.

- Never, under any circumstances, beat or shake a child. If you feel tempted to do so, go seek help immediately.

FINDING A CAREGIVER

"Mom, it's me, Juanita. You won't believe what that little bitch Melanie did. We left a voice-activated tape recorder under the couch in the playroom. She was taking care of Jason last night, and because he spilled his juice, she yelled at him for almost a minute. He started sobbing, and she just yelled louder. Then it took her another five minutes to calm him down! When we got home, she told us that everything had gone just fine. I just called to tell her we won't be calling her again. God, it could have led to something much worse if we hadn't taped her!"

"Juanita, take it easy. I can help you make sure that never happens again."

"How can you do that?"

"When MaryBeth went back to work last month, she asked me if my friends or I knew any nannies. We didn't. Well, you know how I love the Internet, so I went online to find one in this area, and I discovered a whole bunch of sites that tell you what to do. I didn't tell you about it, because I thought you were happy with Melanie. So let me get my download stuff. I've underlined the best ideas, and I'll read them to you over the phone, okay?"

"Great."

"Okay, here are the most important points. First, if you want somebody really good, it could take you a couple of months. I know that's a long time, but if you really want Jason to be safe, you have a lot of work to do. You have to get several recommendations, from either friends or agencies, and then carefully check on each candidate. Try to talk to anyone who knows the person, even those who aren't references. See if the references show any significant interruptions in work history, and if so, find out why. You might want to go to a search engine to see if the people you're interviewing are really who they say they are. You can call the police to see if there are any complaints or warrants out on them. You really should go online to make sure they're not on any sexual offender lists. You need to verify everything on their résumés."

"Do you really think it's necessary to do all that, Mom?"

"These experts say you need to develop a 'healthy paranoia' if you want to be confident Jason is being cared for well. Like you said yourself, Juanita, you don't want a repeat of Melanie. And that's not all. You ought to watch the interaction between Jason and each of these people. Don't be biased against a man; women can be just as mean as men, and men can be just as kind as women."

"I'm thinking of installing one or two nannycams, those little round cameras that hook up to a computer. What do you think of that?"

"Well, there are two opinions on that. It might catch a bad person in the act, but they also could do what they do in a room where you don't have a camera. Also, it can interfere with a sense of trust you want to build up. All of this is up to you, of course, but most of it makes sense to me."

"Mom, thanks a million. I'll let you know how it goes."

HOW TO PICK THE RIGHT CAREGIVER FOR YOUR CHILD

Many parents are faced with the task of trying to find a caregiver to leave their child with. Here are some tips for helping you find the right person:

- Request references from the parents of other children the applicants have recently taken care of, and call each of the parents.
- Ask what training they've had, and look into the validity of it.
- Ask what books on child care they have read.
- Find out if they are CPR certified.
- Make sure they have a valid driver's license.
- Discuss with them how they will discipline your child when she acts up.

Once you select a caregiver:

- Post all contact telephone numbers on the refrigerator.
- Alert the caretaker if your child has any allergies.
- Let the person know your child's routines.
- Explain what to do if your child gets hurt.
- Make sure the caretaker knows how to maintain a safe environment while watching your child.
- Let the caretaker know where you are going and what time you will be back.
- Let the caretaker know your policy of having guests or other children over.
- Call home every few hours to check in.

TEACHER ABUSE OF STUDENTS

Schools are not always the safe havens for children that they should be. Rarely, but still too often, those who represent the authorities in schools are themselves the cause of abuse. Researchers estimate that as many as one in ten students is sexually harassed or psychologically or physically abused by a teacher or school worker at some point in their academic career. A 2000 survey of students in eighth through eleventh grades reported that 9.6 percent of students had experienced some kind of abuse by teachers or other school employees.

Over the past ten years, there has been a rise in the number of allegations of abuse against teachers. According to a report put out by a teacher support organization, between three hundred and five hundred allegations of abuse are made each year against teachers; less than 5 percent (fifteen to twenty-five cases) are proven in court. Most often, allegations appear to center on female teachers and male students. A case that made headlines was a thirteen-year-old male student and his female teacher who were involved in sexual activities. The teacher has been charged with fifteen counts, and it is believed that the sexual activity occurred both on school grounds and at the teacher's car and home. The case was recently resolved, with the teacher found guilty on all counts yet sentenced only to probation. This has raised questions about whether sexual abuse by a female is regarded as serious as that by a male.

Also making headlines are incidents of abuse of high school athletes by coaches. It is hard to obtain data, especially on psychological or physical abuse, because the line between legitimate criticism and abuse isn't always easy to define. Kansas State University researcher Robert Shoop makes the following suggestions on this subject: "Coaches or teachers shouldn't be going over to their students' house after school. They shouldn't be buying them presents; they shouldn't be making phone calls to them at night. And the students should know that when any of these things happen, it's inappropriate; a red flag should be raised" (Tippin, 2003). Shoop also finds that "there is some data that says the perpetrator does not pick a child who rejects their first contact," such as a touch or inappropriate language, and instead moves on to another student.

Headlines about abuse by teachers, administrators, and coaches seem to be making the nightly news regularly, and they can leave you fearing that this could happen to your children. Here are some suggested actions to help prevent your child from becoming a victim of abuse at school.

How to Prevent Abuse by School Personnel

- Talk to your children about the school personnel with whom they come in contact. Ask the children if they feel comfortable talking with their teachers if they need help with their school work. Also, ask if a teacher has ever done anything that has made them feel uncomfortable. Abuse can include more subtle aggression, such as mocking by the teacher, restriction of bathroom "privileges," and threatening looks, all of which might be explained away by an abusive educator.

- There are types of physical abuse that often don't get reported to parents, such as pinching, shaking, and pulling children by the ears; using fear-inducing techniques to control children; and tipping or pulling chairs out from under seated children.

- Talk with other parents in your child's class if you suspect something may be going on between a student and the teacher.

- Ask to monitor your children's classrooms from time to time. True, most parents do not have a lot of time to devote to this precaution, but usually you can tell in five minutes whether the atmosphere in the classroom is tense and foreboding or relaxed and conducive to learning. If the former, you should stay longer and watch carefully.

- When you go to parent-teacher meetings, don't just listen to the teacher's prepared remarks about your child. Have a few questions of your own that are aimed at getting at the teacher's values—for example, "What's your view on managing misbehavior?" and "What techniques are you likely to use to shape your pupil's values?"

- Educational abuse isn't limited to teachers. You need to check on your child's relationships with coaches, tutors, club leaders, counselors, and volunteer personnel.

- It is a sad commentary on the current situation, but most teachers and coaches know that they are ill advised to hug, pat the arm, or in any other way touch a student, even if that student is emotionally upset. If you do hear of any school personnel touching your children, investigate immediately. It might be innocent, but it is a warning sign, just as are phone calls a teacher or coach makes to your child at home, invitations to an educator's home, or presents they give.

WHEN HER DAUGHTER STARTED DATING

Soonyi is a strong-willed woman. She was born a few years after the Korean War ended, and as a result, much of her adolescence was shaped by the war and its aftermath in Seoul. Although Soonyi was the third of six daughters, she became the female head of the household because her mother was too frail to assume the duties, and neither of her older sisters was able or willing.

Being a family leader meant that Soonyi learned to manage the household at an early age. Her father was the breadwinner, but when he brought his paychecks home, it was Soonyi who figured out how best to spend the money. This responsibility was suitable for Soonyi because she has outstanding analytical and organizational skills, and disorder has always bothered her.

Similar rigidity was present at the American army base that remained in Korea after the war. Soonyi admired the army's orderly and systematic training, marches, and scheduling. She and one of her sisters spent a lot of time observing the friendly American GIs who marched by their house on occasion. However, she was hesitant around "those Americans" because it was difficult to erase a vivid memory that haunted Soonyi regularly. Once or twice a GI had made unwanted sexual advances toward her sister. Soonyi was stronger than her sister and didn't allow others to take advantage of her. Eventually Soonyi fell in love with and married one of the GIs. She knew her husband, Patrick, wouldn't do anything inappropriate or out of line.

Soonyi and Patrick returned to the United States shortly after being married, and soon had two daughters. Soonyi raised her children with an expert hand, although it soon became clear that her love of discipline and order was preventing her from having a close relationship with them.

Unfortunately, Soonyi did not know how to be otherwise. She had been a commandant for so long that she could not figure out how to be a warm, loving, and forgiving mother. Instead, she acted as a full-time disciplinarian, giving herself the sole authority to create and enforce the rules of the household.

Today Soonyi's older daughter is fourteen years old and part of an after-school program organized by the local college. Every day when Annie comes home, she excitedly talks about the "cute college boys" who are so helpful. Soonyi worries that her daughter is vulnerable to being sexually molested by one of the young men. Soonyi knew she had to suppress her initial reaction to remove Annie immediately from the program. Yet she knew something had to be done.

One afternoon the phone rang. It was Ellen, Soonyi's closest and dearest friend. Ellen knew of Soonyi's concern for Annie's safety because the two frequently discussed the topic. Ellen had uncovered some startling facts earlier that day while volunteering at a local health clinic and wanted to share her findings with Soonyi.

Ellen rustled through her purse and found the scrap paper where she had jotted down some notes:

- A survey of eighth and ninth graders found that 25 percent reported they had been victims of some kind of dating violence, and 8 percent of these had been sexually abused.
- Younger girls report the most severe violence.
- In a survey of 232 high school students, 16 percent reported some degree of sexual victimization by a dating partner within the past year.

Ellen immediately sensed Soonyi's growing discomfort; however, along with these disheartening facts, Ellen also had found simple rules for kids to follow to prevent abuse.

- Do not be afraid to use the word no. If someone asks for a hug or wants you to sit on his or her lap and you are not interested, just say no.
- If anyone, even someone you know, wants to give you a kiss and you feel uncomfortable, tell the person you want to shake hands instead.

Soonyi wanted to discuss Annie's relationship with "cute older boys" with her daughter immediately. This proved to be very difficult: Annie knew her mother as an authoritarian figure who did not talk much about feelings. Even attempting to talk about this sensitive issue would be a challenge.

That afternoon when Annie came home from her after-school program, Soonyi sat her down and as gently and honestly as she could explained her concerns. Soonyi felt relieved to have opened a line of communication with her daughter and hoped that Annie would know how much she loved her and worried about her, even if Soonyi wasn't always able to display it as openly as she would like.

DATE RAPE

Dating violence is defined by the U.S. Department of Justice as "the perpetration or threat of an act of violence by at least one member of an unmarried couple on the other member within the context of dating or courtship." It can occur between same-sex couples as well, and women ages sixteen to twenty-four are most often victimized; the incidence is twenty in a thousand women.

Date rape and less serious forms of dating abuse are often preventable. A few precautions are necessary.

What You Can Do to Prevent Date Rape

- Recognize the early warning signs that a dating partner may eventually become abusive:

    Extreme jealousy

    Controlling behavior

    Alcohol and drug use

    Explosive anger

    Efforts to isolate the partner from friends and family

    Being alert for these signs and ending the relationship go a long way toward keeping safe.

- Ask your children to make a compact with themselves as to what they will and will not allow in a relationship. It is essential that they make these standards known to a date before going out and that they be assertive in sticking to their rules.

- Tell your children to trust their suspicions. It's "better to be rude than wrong."

- When either partner on a date drinks or uses drugs, trouble may lie ahead. Even if your child knows the person he or she

is dating well, substance use can turn the date into an occasion of date rape. If both partners partake, the odds in favor of
trouble are more than doubled.

Just thinking about the possibilities presented in this chapter is
often upsetting for parents and children alike. We remind you to
avail yourselves of the suggested activities in Chapters Ten and
Eleven to relieve this problem.

8

SCHOOL VIOLENCE

"You Won't Put My Son by the Windows, Will You?"

For some children, violence in school is a minor issue, whereas for others, daily violence is a very real possibility. Since the tragedy at Columbine High School, we are much more aware of the possibility that such a catastrophe could strike again. But what are the chances that your child will experience a violent act at school? Is Columbine a true reflection of the real danger? Let's look at the data.

SOME FACTS ABOUT SCHOOL VIOLENCE

If you can imagine that the facts about violence in schools were posted on the side of a cereal box, the warning panel would look exactly like Figure 8.1. As you can see, the most extreme forms of violence are rare. Nevertheless, the threat of violence can keep students away from school, prevent them from going to after-school events, and leave them in fear every day. Here are some signs that your child is being victimized by violence at school:

- Fascination with weapons or violence
- Cruelty to pets or other animals
- Obsession with violent games and TV shows
- Bringing a weapon of any kind to school
- Behaving like a bully

FIGURE 8.1. School Violence Facts

School Violence Facts	
Overall Injurious Incidents to	
Children in U.S.—2003	171,000
% affected	18
By category	*% affected*
Physical bullying by students	
Punching	15
Slapping	17
Shoving	19
Armed violence by students	
Knives, threatened	13
Knives, stabbings	4
Clubs, sticks	11
Guns, threatening	7
Guns, shootings	2
Abuse by a teacher	
Physical	7
Emotional	11

- School phobia
- Self-image of a victim
- Art or writing that reflects depression
- Wanting to be alone a lot

PLEASE DON'T PUT MY SON BY THE WINDOWS!

Rita Gorelli had just dropped off Tony, her third grader, at school. As she walked toward her car, she turned and looked back at the school, hoping to catch sight of him sitting at his desk by the window in his classroom. But when she did spot his curly-haired head, her heart began to race as a terrifying image went through her mind. She could almost see a terrorist on one knee shooting up at the windows along the side of the building. Tony would be one of the first to be shot. Most of the other children would be safer because they were away from the window, protected from being hit by the upward angle of the deadly spray of bullets.

When this possibility occurred to Rita, she hurried back into her son's classroom and immediately asked that he be moved to a desk against the inner wall. "What for?" the teacher asked.

"I just can't bear to think of how vulnerable Tony is now," Rita replied. "Please, it isn't much to ask."

"But I can't imagine what it is that you think is threatening him."

"Don't you see," Rita cried. "If some madman decides to shoot at the building from out there in the parking lot, Tony will be right in the line of fire! So please, move him over there, or I'll take this to the principal."

"But Mrs. Gorelli, if I move him, I will have to tell him why. Do you want me to say it's for the reason you just gave me? Don't you think that would just scare him? What if he tells the other students about this? That would scare them and make them all want to sit by the wall. Some of them would be too frightened even to walk by the windows! I'm sorry, but I feel this is over the top. If you disagree with what I'm saying, maybe you should take this to the principal."

Rita knew that the chances of a terrorist attack on this particular school were minuscule. She knew she was being extreme in asking for this change. But if there was even the smallest possibility that it would occur, she believed she had to try and prevent it.

ACTIONS TO TAKE AGAINST SCHOOL VIOLENCE

Knowing what to do about school violence is especially difficult because it involves so many other people. Fortunately, it is not necessary for you to control everyone. What is most important, and where you can have immediate impact, is the control you exert over your own behavior and the direct and indirect influence you have on your children.

Keeping Your Child Safe in School

- Know your children's friends. The best way to do this is to make your house attractive to those friends. Strike up conversations with them, and ask them questions about what's happening at school. They may tell you things they won't tell their own parents and that your children may not want to tell you.

- Join with other parents through school and neighborhood associations, religious organizations, civic groups, and youth activity groups. Work with them to develop standards for school-related events, acceptable out-of-school activities, and adult supervision.

- Set clear limits on your children's behaviors. Discuss punishments and rewards in advance too. Consistent discipline helps teach self-discipline.

- Volunteer in your child's classroom, library, or in after-school activities.

- Check to see if your children's schools have a "Safe School Plan" and that the teachers are fully trained to respond to emergencies.

- Talk to your children in a calm manner about what to do if a violent incident occurs at their school. Ensure that they understand the school's plan. If your child feels a rule is wrong, discuss his or her reasons and what rule might work better.

- There's nothing like being a role model. Settle your own conflicts with your partner peaceably, and manage anger without violence.

Keeping Your Child Safe from Armed Violence

- Never keep any type of firearms in your home. More Americans are killed by guns each year than by all other methods combined. In many states, parents can be held liable for their children's actions, including inappropriate use of firearms.

- If you feel the need to keep firearms at home, ensure that they are securely locked, that ammunition is locked and stored separately, and that children know weapons are never to be touched without your express permission and supervision.

- The Gun-Free Schools Act (GFSA) requires a minimum one-year expulsion for students who bring firearms to school. Although GFSA is not a zero-tolerance law, many school policies enacted in response to it are often referred to as "zero tolerance." In most cases, that means if your child brings a weapon to school, expulsion will follow immediately.

- Many of the children who bring weapons to school start out as verbal bullies. Educate your children about bullying and how this behavior affects the victims.

- Most fistfights and fights involving weapons happen after school. Make sure after-school activities are constructive and healthy and supervised by adults.

- Your children should be aware of other kids talking about violence. For example, teach them to go to a teacher and you immediately after hearing about any discussion of planned violence, even if they are convinced that those kids are just joking.

- If you hear rumors, get the facts. Because of all the publicity around school violence, schools may have a tendency to overreact.

THE MOST RECENT PROBLEM: INAPPROPRIATE BLOGS

A blog is a personal journal on a Web site that is available to anyone to read and respond to. Anyone who wants to present his or her views to the general public easily can set up such a site, and some have become enormously popular. The problem is that when teens write blogs, they often make the mistake of assuming that only their close friends will bother to go to the site. Thus, they tend to be more revealing about their lives than is prudent.

This can lead to two unwanted results. Sometimes child abusers surf for blogs and then use the personal details to inveigle themselves into a teen's confidence for nefarious purposes. More often, in a desire to express innermost thoughts and feelings, the young bloggers expose themselves to the judgments and criticism of any fellow student who feels like reading the site. A few bloggers, in their eagerness to be noticed, go over the top: they make up bizarre stories about themselves or they upload pictures of themselves in underwear or less. To find out whether your child is a blogger, simply type his or her name in the search box of your browser; if there is a site, you will find it and can judge for yourself whether it is appropriate.

CHARACTER ASSASSINATION BY INTERNET

From time to time throughout the past fourteen years, Ann has found herself saying little prayers of thanks to God for her daughter, Denise. The girl has been nearly perfect: cooperative, loving, funny, pretty. Having her for a daughter has made Ann think of herself as an excellent parent. She has always known there is such a thing as good luck, but she must be doing something right. For a person whose own childhood was "hardly a bed of roses," as she describes it to Denise, this experience has done wonders for her self-respect.

To be honest, that is why every time she thinks about the present situation, it literally causes her to feel nauseated. Of course, she sympathizes tremendously with the agonies fourteen-year-old Denise has been enduring too. It has been hurtful for both of them.

It began innocently enough. Since she shares nearly everything of interest about school with her mother, Denise had asked Ann to read the instant message to her large group of Internet friends, most of them also in the ninth grade at Emerson High: "Guess what Emerson ninth grader is having you know what kind of sex with Demetrius Anopoulos? She's been meeting him almost every day after school for a little session in the family room at his house. Stay tuned!"

Ann had taken it as an opportunity to talk to her daughter about her own sexual knowledge, attitudes, and values. It worked well; their discussion ranged freely and ended with a sense of satisfaction for them both. Their happiness was short-lived. The next day an IM delivered the following information: "So, did you guess who our class slut is? Of course you did. It's always the quiet ones, isn't it? Yes, in spite of her 'good girl' front, Demetrius's love slave is none other than Denise Bellaroni! Yeah, she acts like everybody's friend, but watch out for your boyfriend. If she goes after him, he's a goner. The fake little bitch!"

Denise screamed when she read the message. Ann came running, and Denise pointed to the screen. When she finished, Ann almost screamed too. As the shock receded, the thought struck: "Could this possibly be true?" She hated herself for suspecting, but she couldn't imagine how or why someone could make up such a story. When she questioned her daughter about the situation, she quickly realized the story was false. Nevertheless, Denise's feelings were hurt that her mother had even suspected her.

When school officials were shown the two messages, they called in the police officer assigned to the school district. He interviewed everyone in the group, and it became obvious to him that the perpetrator was a girl named Nadia. Demetrius had turned her down when she had asked him to go on a date with her. He told her he liked Denise and was planning to try and start something up with her. Nadia was so furious that she made up the story to hurt him. She enjoyed trying to shoot Denise down because Nadia hated her "goody-goody" persona. Nevertheless, Nadia insisted that she was innocent.

The principal sent out a message to everyone on the instant message list, explaining his belief that someone had falsely accused Denise. Demetrius backed her, but nothing could be proved one way or the other, and Nadia's friends still believed her. The harm to Denise was done: a number of class-mates now refused to talk to her, and the deep trust between Denise and her mother had been shaken. And Nadia wasn't through with her either: Denise was too tempting a target for the angry girl's general resentments against the world.

But there was an even greater victim in this dangerous scenario: the group itself. Most of the members quickly under-stood how easy it would be to "get" someone who had offended them. They could also see that they themselves could become a target for very little reason, and there would be nothing they could do to defend themselves.

BULLYING: HOW TO SPOT IT, AND WHAT TO DO ABOUT IT

Bullying occurs when one student says nasty and unpleasant things to another; when one student hits, kicks, threatens, locks inside a room, or sends nasty notes to another; or when no one ever talks to a child. Students can behave in the roles of a bully, a victim, a bully-victim, or a bystander. A survey of nearly sixteen thousand students in grades 6 through 10 across the United States found that about one-third reported frequent involvement in bullying. These were about evenly distributed with bullies, victims, and bully-victims. As astounding as it might seem, 6 million boys and 4 million girls are in-volved in a fight on school grounds every year. The stakes are high:

the Secret Service has discovered that 71 percent of school shooters had themselves been targets of a bully.

In recent years, bullying has become a serious hot topic. In part, this is because girls are becoming as likely to bully as boys, though they are more likely than boys to bully in a group. And bullying is becoming more common. About 25 percent of all children have been bullied at least once during their childhoods, either mentally or physically.

Many times, it is fairly obvious that a child has been bullied: there are bruises, cuts, and torn clothing that are easy to spot. Psychological markers are harder to detect. Those indicators include

- Headaches, stomach pains before school
- Poor appetite, especially on Sunday nights
- Poor grades
- Decline from usual activities
- Not having many friends
- Emotional signs of stress: anxiety, depression, fear, anger, nervousness
- Better relationships with adults than with children

When a child is bullied by a classmate, the typical reaction is fear. Over 160,000 students miss school every day in fear of attack by a bully. The middle school years are when most of the bullying occurs. In fact, bullying increases in elementary school, peaks in middle school, and diminishes in high school. Seven percent of eighth graders stay home at least once a month due to bullies. Even more students say they are scared throughout the entire school day, and a significant number of students drop out of school because of repeated bullying.

An overwhelming 80 percent of the time, bullying escalates from verbal to physical. It is a fair estimate to say that elementary-aged children use more verbal abuse among themselves, but usually beginning around age twelve, children become more likely to use physical abuse, such as kicking, choking, or fighting.

The average bullies come from middle-class homes, have un-usually low self-esteem, and are exceptionally angry. Manifestations of anger such as setting fires or torturing animals are likely predic-tors of a child's becoming a bully in middle or high school. As of late, a quarter of high school students have reported carrying a weapon to school for protection.

Although schools are becoming more aware of statistics and most are taking measures to reduce bullying, there is quite a lot you and your family can do to protect children from this frightening affliction.

Keeping Your Child Safe from Bullying

- Learn the signs that indicate your child has been bullied.

- Ask your children's teachers if your children show signs of being a bully.

- Educate your children about being kind to children who do not fit in or are in some way different.

- Discourage name-calling and teasing, behaviors that often escalate into fistfights. Whether the teaser is violent or not, the victim may see violence as the only way to stop it. Have no tolerance for your children's participating in fistfights and name-calling.

- Help your children learn how to examine and find solutions to problems. Kids who know how to approach a problem and resolve it effectively are less likely to be angry or frustrated.

- Make sure that your children's teachers are doing what they can to foster respectful interactions among their students and are speaking out against teasing and other behaviors consis-tent with bullying.

- Help your children avoid high-risk areas at their schools, such as tunnels, or other isolated areas.

- Countermand the myth that being aggressive is manly or admirable.

INTERNET BULLYING

Alex was being teased by a group of girls in his school about his diminutive stature. Although Alex was small for his age, his parents never saw it as an issue, and they weren't aware that some of his classmates were mocking him about it over the Internet. It wasn't until after Alex used his grandfather's antique shotgun to kill himself that his parents realized the extent of the problem. Alex had begged these kids to leave him alone, but they wouldn't. They knew he was contemplating suicide, and they dared him to. It was all a big joke to them. Alex's mother summed up the tragedy: "If someone is picking on you in the school yard, you can go home. When it's on the computer at home, you have nowhere else to go!"

Children who watch a lot of TV are more likely to become bullies later in school; the more TV they watch, the more likelihood of their bullying. Researchers have found this correlation as early as four years old. If you want to raise children who won't bully, limit television watching, read to them instead. Here are some other tips for dealing with Internet bullying:

- Be sure to save the cyberbullying messages as evidence.
- Meet with school officials to help resolve allegations that cyberbullying has occurred, whether your child is the target or the alleged perpetrator.
- If threats are made, call the police and the Internet service provider.
- Keep user profiles general, and do not post photographs.
- If the messages are threatening, contact school or police officials.
- Instruct your children to change their screen names regularly, and give them only to people they trust.

- Teach your children never to post anything they wouldn't want others to read.

"HELICOPTER MOMS"

Although we counsel you to keep up to date about what is happening in your children's classroom, it is easy to overdo it. Mothers who do are called "helicopter moms"—at least many teachers call them that. The term refers to mothers who seem to hover over their children, trying always to protect them from real or imagined dangers.

Many schools, especially those in upper-middle-class communities, are being overwhelmed with volunteers for room mothers and teacher assistants. Some of these aides are more trouble than help. Teachers describe two troublesome types: "smotherers," who believe that only their presence can keep their child safe, and "micromanagers," who want their children to be successful and want to organize the school climate so that it always fosters that goal.

Increasing class size has made more and more mothers to want to intervene in their children's behalf. Unfortunately, the result tends to be angry, defensive teachers who feel they are being spied on by parents who don't trust them. The solution? A balanced approach. Ask yourself this question: "Am I volunteering because I want to help all the children, or only mine?" And if you find yourself packing your own school lunch when you pack your children's, you may be overdoing it!

There is no denying that the atmosphere in schools is not as benign as it was when most of us were children. Some say that the quality of teaching, and especially classroom control, has dropped since opportunities for careers in a multitude of other fields have opened up for women since the 1960s. Others blame the media. Still others blame more permissive child-rearing practices. By no means does this exhaust the list of candidates for blame. Whatever the reason, children are more at risk for getting injured, seduced, or hooked than they were fifty years ago when fights rarely involved weapons, and seduction by computer and drugs was unheard of.

In fact, the media make us so much more aware of what does happen that most of us have an exaggerated idea of the seriousness of the problem. As the statistics presented in this chapter reveal, the vast percentage of children are quite safe from all but innocuous injury. In schools, perhaps more than any other area, overreaction can be costly: it frightens the children, alienates teachers, and exacerbates your own anxieties. Follow the suggestions in this chapter, and ask for the serenity to accept the acceptable risk that is unavoidable.

9

MAKING YOUR HOUSE SAFE

"Where Are the Dangerous Places?"

Accidental injuries in the home have become an increasingly serious health problem in the United States. They are the leading cause of death for individuals between the ages of one and forty-four and the fifth leading cause of death in the United States. More than eighteen thousand accidental deaths of children at home occur in this country every year. Of all nonfatal unintentional injury events, 42 percent occur in the home, translating to nearly 12 million nonfatal home injuries annually. In addition, emergency departments treat more than 10 million such injuries.

Burns are the most common causes of childhood accidental fatalities in the home. Infants and toddlers are especially likely to be victims of drowning, inhalation of dangerous fumes, and suffocation. Males are more prone to accidents than females.

On average, the home is the most dangerous place for children. For one thing, it is the place where they spend the largest percentage of their time. For another, there are many threats lurking there. Happily, it is also the place where a few simple precautions will yield the greatest payoff. The first step in protecting your family at home is to discuss safety issues with them, mainly how to prevent injuries and what to do in case an injury occurs. Communication, especially before an emergency happens, can prevent it from becoming a disaster.

ACTIONS TO TAKE AGAINST DANGERS IN THE HOME

Here are some of the best ideas for keeping your family safe while at home. Many of these tips may seem like common sense, and they are, but experts say they are also the ones most likely to be overlooked. Carefully reading and carrying out these suggestions will help you to feel calmer about the threats in your world.

General Tips

- Develop an emergency plan for weather crises like the one offered in Chapter Two and a plan for dealing with a terrorist attack, offered in Chapter Four.

- Make a map of your house, showing danger areas and places where safety equipment is kept. An example of how to make such a map also appears later in this chapter.

- Specialized plans for holidays and summertime are detailed later in this chapter and offer models for other safety routines you and your family may want to design.

- If you have heating, cooking, or power equipment that uses fuels such as oil, natural gas, coal, wood, propane, or gasoline, your home is at risk for potential carbon monoxide poisoning. Homes with attached garages are also at risk, because vehicles left running in the garage can cause gases to seep into the home. Poisoning can be prevented by proper care and use of alarms that provide early detection of leaks or accumulation.

- Install smoke alarms on every level of your home and near every sleeping area.

- A grandparent's house may not be as childproof as your own home. You may not do things the way your parents do, but that needn't be a cause for conflict. You should tell them that although they did a good job of raising you, new discoveries suggest things may be safer if they are done a bit differently. You and your parents need to confer about what is expected of the children, and the children themselves need to be explicitly prepared for life at their grandparents' house.

- Look for warnings on product labels that provide important safety information about use of the product.

- Hold family fire drills frequently and at various times so your escape plans become second nature.

- To prevent confusion, never store nonfood products with food products. Also, you do not want any hazardous substances to leave residue that might contaminate your food.

- Dispose of any expired prescriptions and medicine by flushing them down the toilet. Do not leave them in the garbage where children or pets could find them.

- Do not leave any medicinal substances or supplies in places that are accessible to children, such as bathroom drawers, nightstands, or purses. Store medicine in locked cabinets.

- Identify and remedy anything in your home that could interfere with your leaving quickly in an emergency, including windows that are stuck, heavy furniture blocking an exit, and broken or dangerous locks.

- Never store gasoline indoors. Because of its highly flammable nature, keep only small amounts in an approved container.

- Handle all chemicals and other potentially hazardous materials in a safe manner. Always keep them in their original container.

- Never mix household substances. Some products react adversely when they are combined.

- Purchase rope or aluminum fire escape ladders for upstairs bedrooms.

- Especially when working with harsh cleaners or chemicals, wear protective gloves.

- Always stay in the kitchen when food is cooking on the stove.

- Make sure that all surfaces in the kitchen are cleaned and disinfected thoroughly, especially after working with raw foods such as chicken, beef, fish, and eggs. Also, always use a food thermometer to check that food is fully cooked to prevent foodborne illness, which is responsible for over five thousand deaths every year in the United States. You do not want anyone to fall victim to food poisoning.

- Always keep a well-assembled disaster supply kit. Common items to include are water, nonperishable food, a manual can opener, radio, flashlights, batteries, extra cash, and identification. (For more details, refer to Chapter Two on preparing for a weather emergency.)

- Have a fully stocked first-aid kit on hand to treat any injuries in your home that you feel capable of handling.

- Get training in CPR and first aid, especially when you have children. Some accidents require immediate attention.

- Keep a list of emergency telephone numbers in a location that everyone is aware of and is easily accessible. You may want to post a copy near every telephone in the house and make sure they are stored in everyone's cell phones.

- Stay aware of recalled products by visiting www.recalls.gov to make sure that any harmful products you may have in your home are disposed of immediately.

TINY FINGERS IN GREAT DANGER

Maureen Stephanowski cares a lot about home safety. She has four children under the age of eight, and there are such differences in safety issues at each of the different age levels. Seven-year-old Ralph loves to climb things. Once when he was two and a half, she discovered him on top of the refrigerator. The door was open, and it was clear that he had managed to use the shelves inside and on the door to boost himself to this dangerously high spot. She worries about finding him on the roof someday.

Six-year-old Nancy enjoys placing small objects in her ears and nose just to see what will happen. She's had to go to the hospital on two occasions. The removal of the inserted items was rather unpleasant, but that hasn't stopped her from her trying it again.

Three-year-old Ben is fascinated by bottles and boxes. He cannot resist pulling them from under the sink and opening them to learn what is inside. She keeps poisonous ingredients on a top shelf of the pantry, but Maureen worries that some-day she will overlook one and he will get to it.

She is most concerned about the baby of the family, one-year-old Debbie. An early crawler, the toddler is already on the verge of running. And she is into everything, her mind a web of bins into which she loves to store information. As the result of seeing a television advertisement on toddler safety, Maureen installed covers on every electrical socket in the house that is less than three feet off the floor. She thought that would do it (the commercial had promised it would). In fact, the little plug-in caps did not protect curious Debbie's tiny fingers from exploring the sockets.

Worse, perhaps imitating her older sister, the child had put one of the caps into her mouth. Maureen was alerted to the peril when she heard a strange, soft thud that seemed to come from the living room. Some instinct made her dash from the kitchen, to find Debbie on the floor, unconscious, her face slightly blue. Luckily Maureen had read about the Heimlich maneuver, the procedure in which pressure is applied to the abdomen of a person who has an object blocking the passage of breath in the throat. Two pushes, and the cap was expelled. The doctor to whom Debbie was taken said that she was fine and urged that the caps be replaced. He mentioned a new type that is permanently fixed to the socket by the screw that holds the face plate in place.

"Fine," thought Maureen, "but what's next? Is there no end to the things a mother must think of to keep her children safe? The job is simply overwhelming!"

The answer to Maureen's question is: yes, there is an end to it. Do the things in this book, and then try to get yourself and your family to feel confident that you've done a reasonable job of keeping yourselves safe. Here are additional safety tips, arranged by age group.

Tips for Infants and Young Children

- Cover all safety outlets with caps that screw into the outlet. Children can remove the plug-in types and swallow them.

- Gate off the tops and bottoms of every staircase to avoid a spill.

- Look for "washable/hygienic materials" or similar labeling on stuffed toys and dolls and "flame retardant/flame resistant" labeling on fabric products and costumes.

- Keep containers of small candies or any other objects that pose a choking hazard out of reach.

- Find a safe spot (not under the kitchen sink) for cleaners and liquids that children cannot access.

- Make sure appliances on tables and counters do not have cords dangling off the side so children can grab them.

- Keep all knives and other sharp objects in places where children cannot access them.

- Cover areas under and around play equipment with soft materials such as hardwood chips, mulch, pea gravel, and sand (materials should be nine to twelve inches deep and extend six feet from all sides of play equipment).

- Identify the locations of dangerous substances in such places as the bathroom, kitchen, garage, and shed. All of these materials should be properly secured out of the reach of children, preferably in high places. Make sure that all of these products have childproof seals on them.

Tips for Protecting Teens

- Don't leave unfinished alcoholic beverages around where curious teens might find and try them.

- Of course, you shouldn't smoke around children, but if you do, make sure not to leave dirty ashtrays around where kids might try to smoke the extinguished butts.

- Leave your parents with a list of the same emergency numbers and instructions as you would leave any other person who would be caring for your children.

- Cabinets that store potentially harmful materials should have locks on them, especially if you have adolescent children.

- Keep substances in their original containers to prevent confusion and to maintain any specific safety instructions to consult if an accident occurs involving the substance.

MAPPING YOUR HOUSE FOR SAFETY

With your children, make a map of your house that indicates potential places of danger and of safety. To do this, you will need several large sheets of paper and three or more colored markers. The age of your children will determine how much preparation you need for this activity. If your children are unable to represent spaces figuratively, you will need to prepare a floor plan of your house ahead of time. Older children can create their own maps at whatever degree of complexity they are able. Alternatively, you might want to make your map on a computer, using the drawing function of your word processor or commercial map-making software.

Up to a point, the larger your map is, the better in terms of the amount of visible detail. A map the size of poster board paper (about two by four feet) is good. You might also try to emulate the way architects draw blueprints. When your map is created, walk around the house with it, and identify locations of possible danger. You might want to look for places that a young cousin could hurt herself if she were to visit—for instance, a fireplace, a screen door opening onto a deck, and exposed outlets. Have the children mark these with one color.

Now go through the house again, this time looking for places of safety. On every floor, mark in a color different from that you used to represent danger such locations as phones, a first-aid kit, ice cubes (for sprains), and fire ladders or outside stairs. Finally, with a third color, draw a fire escape route on the map, with the routes from bedrooms leading to a meeting place outside the house. Use other marker colors to add any other features on your map that you think are important.

This activity will draw your attention to possible hazards and increase your awareness of how much your children know about safety. This should have the added benefit of putting your mind more at ease.

SEASONAL SAFETY

Every season brings with it special hazards. We have covered three of them in the sections that follow (Halloween, springtime, and summertime), but you might want to draw up your own lists for the other seasons.

Halloween

Although Halloween is one of the holidays that kids enjoy the most, the Home Safety Council urges parents to recognize the dangers. Because of the increased hazards that are associated with this holiday, it can become a scary day in more ways than one. There are three main areas that need to be addressed in preparation for

Halloween safety: fires and burns, slips and falls, and choking and poisoning.

Fires and Burns

- Fire departments recommend families not to decorate for Halloween using candles with live flames. The combination of darkness, excitement, and big, flowing costumes does not mix well with candles.

- Use a battery-operated light instead of a candle to illuminate the jack-o'-lantern.

- When using outdoor decorative lighting, never put more than three lights on an extension cord. To avoid a mishap, use only outdoor lights outside and indoor lights inside, and check often for loose connections, broken sockets, and frayed wires.

- Make sure that your kids are not dressed in costumes that are flammable, hinder their sight or movement, or do not fit properly. Avoid floppy hats, long sleeves, masks, and flowing skirts. Oversized costumes can be dangerous.

Slips and Falls

- Make sure that your walkway, sidewalks, driveway, lawn, and stairs are clear of anything that children could trip or slip on, including toys, ornaments, and leaves.

- Keep the path to your house well lit so that nighttime visitors can see where they are going.

- Install handrails that are firmly secure on both sides of the front steps.

- Before you head out for the night with children, apply reflective tape to their costumes, and make sure to bring a flashlight with batteries that work.

- Go with your children on their rounds. Unless you are very confident in them, even teens need to be accompanied because of the increased risks that Halloween presents.

Choking and Poisoning

- Children under the age of three should not be given small candies or foods, like gum, hard candy, or nuts, that can block their airways if swallowed.
- Although you don't want to put a damper on the holiday, inspect your children's candy before they eat it. Do not let your child eat it before returning home. Things to look for include loose wrappers and small pinholes in the candy.

Springtime Holidays: Easter, Passover, and the Spring Equinox

The springtime holiday season is a joyous time when families come together to eat a wonderful meal, participate in fun activities, such as an Easter egg hunt, and spend time with one another. Debra Holtzman, cochair of the Florida SAFE KIDS Coalition, offers these simple ways to help ensure a healthy spring holiday for your family and your pets:

- *Baby chicks.* They may be cute and festive, but baby chicks may also carry Salmonella. Since the risk for infections is higher for children, the Centers for Disease Control and Prevention specifically advises parents not to consider placing chicks in their children's Easter baskets.
- *Easter lilies.* All parts of this plant are toxic to pets and children and can cause serious poisoning or death if ingested.
- *Eggs.* Hard-boiled eggs must be cooked thoroughly to prevent Salmonella contamination. Eggs should be refrigerated no more than two hours after boiling and should be used

within a week, or they should be discarded. Food-safe coloring should be used to dye the eggs. Eggs should not be left hidden for more than two hours. If a long hiding period is necessary, use plastic eggs for your Easter or Equinox egg hunt.

- *Chocolate bunnies.* Chocolate can be fatal to many animals, especially dogs. Be careful not to leave it out where animals can get to it, and remember where you hide everything.

- *Hard candy.* Young children should never be allowed to eat hard candies or other small foods such as popcorn.

- *Pies.* All pies, especially pies with custard, should be refrigerated. If left at room temperature, pies can develop hazardous bacteria.

- *Cookie dough.* If your cookie dough ingredients call for the use of raw egg, do not eat any dough before it is cooked. Otherwise you are at risk for the severe foodborne illness Salmonella.

- *Guests' allergies.* Before guests arrive, ask them whether they are allergic to anything.

- *Perishable foods.* Perishable foods like raw and cooked meat, poultry, and seafood should not be left unrefrigerated for more than two hours. Fruits and vegetables that have been sliced should not remain at room temperature for more than two hours to prevent the formation of bacteria.

- *Alcohol.* All drinks with alcohol, as well as empty and partially empty containers, should be kept completely out of the reach of children. Alcoholic beverages should be stored in a locked cabinet, not in the refrigerator, where they are easily accessible. Children are curious and often imitate their parents, so be careful of the example you set.

- *Cribs.* Especially if you are visiting relatives with your young children, be careful of the crib you place your child in. Make sure that it is not an outdated or recalled product (check www.cpsc.gov). The slat space should measure no more than two and three-eighths inches. If you visit a relative's house and it has an older crib, bring a bumper with you.

Summer Safety

There is a lot of fun to be had in summer, especially by children who are out of school and without worries, but it can also be a time of heightened haphazard behavior that can lead to accidents. Many parents regularly remind their children not to go too deep at the pool or at the beach and to take various other safety precautions when they are away from home. However, many overlook the protection that needs to begin directly in the confines of their own backyard. These threats touch everyone, but young children are especially prone to fall victim to summer mishaps. Fortunately, many of the most common accidents are preventable. The following provides a guide to summer-specific hazards to be aware of:

- Discourage horse-play on decks, porches, roofs, and near open windows. Check to make sure that all screens are securely fitted.

- Keep gardening tools as well as landscaping equipment out of the reach of children. They should never be allowed to operate the equipment alone.

- Survey your backyard for anything that could pose a threat to your children before they play there.

- Make sure that all of your child's vaccines and inoculations (such as tetanus) are up to date.

- Caution must be taken when giving children foods such as hot dogs, peanut butter, lollipops, and candy. Children who are playing should not be allowed to have anything in their mouths. Food should be cut into small pieces, and sticky foods should be avoided. Peanut butter especially can stick to the sides of airways and cause a blockage.

- The summertime can bring about many allergies. Be aware of any characteristic changes in your child's health such as frequently runny noses and watery eyes.

- Teach your children not to tease and play rough with pets.

- Always use bug repellent spray on your children before they go outside. When they come inside, check them for ticks.

- Keep fertilizers and pesticides locked up. Store products in original packaging, so there is no confusion about the contents. If any are exposed to skin or ingested, wash the exposed area with water immediately. Then call Poison Control: 1-800-682–9211.

- Check your yard for poisonous mushrooms or other fungi (they usually appear following a rain), and remove them.

- Learn to identify poison ivy, oak, and sumac. If you see any in your yard, remove it by spraying it with a product available at your hardware or garden store. Never burn it; the acid becomes airborne.

❧

We would like to remind you of the title of our first chapter: *Doing too much is as risky as doing too little*. Please consider including as many of the activities in Chapters Ten and Eleven in your family's precautions as you can. They have been proven to help you avoid the "doing too much" part of our safety equation.

PART TWO

ENSURING YOUR FAMILY'S SERENITY

10

HOW CAN YOUR CHILDREN COPE WITH THEIR FEARS?

Adults often assume childhood is a carefree, happy time, when in fact children are prone to anxious feelings as much as adults are. Moreover, they do not have the life experience to compare new situations to old ones or the ability to make sound judgments about what is worthy of fear and what is fleeting. If parents and others appear anxious or concerned, children are quick to pick up on those cues and internalize the anxiety. As experts regarding your own children, you will likely recognize the symptoms they present when they feel worried about real or imagined situations—perhaps stomachaches, loss of breath, or excess adrenaline. Depending on your children's personalities, you can decide whether physical or mental methods of alleviating anxiety will work best.

In this chapter, we provide sample exercises that you can share with your children. The exercises and activities are based on the COPE technique of alleviating anxiety. Each letter of COPE stands for one strategy that has been shown to reduce anxious feelings and boost creative energy. Depending on the age of your children, you can adapt the activities to meet their developmental level. In many cases, suggestions have been provided for you, but trust your instincts and look to your own experience if you want to make modifications.

C: CALMING THE NERVOUS SYSTEM

The activities in this section are designed to calm the nervous system, the most direct way to alleviate anxiety and gain control over what sometimes may feel like a life-or-death situation. Some activities use physical methods and some mental relaxation. In either case, the end result is a calmer, more focused child.

Know Your Own Heart Rate

One of the quickest and easiest ways to calm down and feel some sense of control in a scary or unpredictable situation is to slow your heart rate. This simple activity is a way for children to focus and regain a healthy heart rate, which will help stem some of their anxiety. Adults can use this exercise as well.

To calculate your child's target heart rate (THR), subtract her age from 220, and then multiply the result by .7 and .85. The two numbers yield the range within which your child's heart rate should fall. When her pulse is taken within five seconds of stopping exercise, it should be somewhere between those two numbers. For example, if your child is ten years old, calculate her THR as follows:

$$220 - 10 = 210$$
$$210 \times .7 = 147$$
$$210 \times .85 = 179$$

Thus, her THR is between 147 and 179.

Take your child's pulse by pressing two fingers into her carotid artery (at the side of the neck) for twenty seconds and counting the heartbeats, then multiply by three. Most children's pulses are between 60 and 80 beats per minute; aerobic exercise usually brings it up to between 140 and 180.

As a means of comparison, have your child do some aerobic activity for twenty to thirty minutes, and take her pulse again. Share the differences with your child, allowing her to see that her pulse rate is significantly higher than it was before she did the aerobic activity. She may be surprised at the difference, and you can remind her that she can lower her rate by taking deep breaths. Take her pulse after a cool-down period as a way to make a final comparison between pulse rates before, during, and after aerobic activity.

Resist, Release, and Relax

This exercise may be done alone or with a partner; the idea is to focus effort and energy on tensing certain muscles as a way of ultimately relaxing them. The sensation of relaxation will be recognized and can then be remembered on future occasions.

Have your child stand in front of you or another partner with her arms at her sides. Place your hands on the child's wrists and hold tightly as your child tries to raise her arms up and outward, so she resembles the letter T. It may be difficult to hold your child's arms down, but try your best to do so while she tries her hardest to raise her arms, for 30 seconds and 60 seconds. Gently let go of your child's arms. They will "float" upward as the tension is released. This floating sensation is something many children find amusing, and they may ask to repeat the exercise.

Show your kids how they can accomplish similar feelings of lightness and floating by standing in a doorway and pushing outward against the frame with their hands. When they push outward for about one minute, they will find that their arms feel light and free when they let go. This is a nice analogy that can be presented to children in terms of letting go of some of the tension we all experience in everyday life.

Ha Ha!

Humor is a terrific tension reliever. This activity provides a way for children to laugh and to get comfortable feeling silly. Sometimes we are afraid to appear foolish in a crisis situation, and the natural instinct is to stifle the impulse to take action. In situations when children's safety may depend on drawing attention to them, this is a fun way to get used to such attention.

You will need to gather several of your children, or several of their friends, because this activity requires at least four children. On a rug or on top of a blanket, have each person lie down on her back with her head resting on the stomach of the next person; the group thus forms a chain of people, heads on stomachs. The group can form a line or circle, depending on how people are more comfortable and the size of the room.

Designate one person to begin. Have that person say the words "Ha Ha!" loudly and boisterously, releasing the sound from the diaphragm. The head of the person whose head is on the speaker's stomach will bounce up and down as the speaker exhales the word "Ha Ha!" The next person in line says "Ha Ha!" followed by the next person, and the next, until everyone has said it, and the pattern continues until, inevitably, everyone is laughing. It is very hard not to laugh when your head is bouncing up and down, and anxious thoughts have a way of disappearing when this happens.

Scale Those Fears

The purpose of this activity is to interrupt anxious moments and reduce their severity. It is a tangible way for children to think about their own thresholds for experiencing anxiety and how situations may contribute to their feelings. They may not even be aware of what was prompting the anxious feelings in the first place. This skill is extremely useful for children who must cope with spontaneous, stressful events during which they are required to act quickly. Children can recall their experience using this activity and draw from their recollections.

Ask your child to describe a situation when she felt extreme panic. Ask her to describe another one that was equally bad. Assign a score of 10 to incidents like that. Now ask her to imagine herself to be completely relaxed. That's level 1. Finally, ask her to think of times when she has felt halfway between those two extremes. Those are level 5 anxieties.

Make up some three- by five-inch cards with the following headings written atop columns across the five-inch side: date, anxiety level number, feelings, and thoughts. Any time your child experiences anxiety above level 3, as soon as possible she should find a private place and fill out a line (or more) on the card. If your child is in the beginning writing stages, she can dictate her feelings for you to write on the cards.

Younger children can refer to scenes from picture books. Ask your child to choose an appealing scene from a favorite book, and then have her pick a scene that she finds frightening. Continue picking scenes of each kind until she has an array of scenes that she can rank from high to low (you can photocopy the illustrations for easy reference). Then discuss with her why she made those choices. As she scales the scenes, you can help her to gain perspective on what situations make her anxious.

Peaceful Pictures, Soothing Slide Show

The ability to visualize is fundamental to anxiety control and draws on all of the senses. First, ask your child to close her eyes and imagine as many as seven scenes that she finds particularly tranquil. Next, request that she write a phrase describing each scene on an index card, and arrange the cards in descending order in terms of their degree of tranquility. With a younger child, have her dictate her ideas to you, or let her choose scenes from pictures in magazines that appeal to her. Your child's list might look like this:

1. Waves on a shore
2. A field of wheat or corn
3. Glowing embers in a fireplace
4. A wildflower meadow

5. A sleeping child in a crib

6. Botanical gardens

7. A neighborhood park

Choose one of the scenes, and ask your child to describe it in greater detail. Go through the list of scenes until she has described each one. Suggest to your child that she memorize the list and practice visualizing each scene. Whenever she feels anxious, she can visualize each scene on the list sequentially, and each step in the "mental slide show" will help her calm down. Visualization helps a child regain calm in the face of stressful events and can provide opportunity for thinking that will help the child choose an appropriate course of action.

O: ORIGINATING AN IMAGINATIVE PLAN

Most anxious children tend to be highly creative. This will come as no surprise to parents whose children come up with seemingly endless lists of things to worry about. Take heart, however, since one of the benefits of having a strong imagination is that it can be used to generate numerous problem-solving strategies to counter fear.

The activities that follow will help you and your child to think more imaginatively and develop ideas for what may help quell some of the anxiety that is produced when your child perceives the environment as unsafe. Although these activities are not actual plans for overcoming anxiety, they will prepare you and your child to develop a plan. In some cases, you may want to alter the instructions or the activity itself to suit your child's personality and learning style.

The Asking Questions Test of Flexibility

The term refers to the ability to see the big picture and not fixate on one aspect of a problem or situation. Young children are not as skilled at this as older children or adults, largely because they have not yet developed the cognitive skills needed to organize pieces of information into categories. Younger children tend to be a bit more rigid in their thinking, so adults who use this activity may need to prompt them more than they do older children.

The purpose of this activity is to get imaginative juices flowing, so try this yourself before you ask your child to respond. With a time limit of five minutes, write down all the questions you can think to ask about the drawing in Figure 10.1—for example, "What's the clown's name?" Do not ask questions that can be asked just by looking at the drawing. Try to ask imaginative questions. Do not read further until you have completed the exercise.

Now score your answers by counting the number of questions you asked that fall into clearly different categories. Analysis of several thousand responses to this test determined that there are twenty categories of questions, which are listed below. Thus, your highest possible score is 20:

Categories for Scoring the Asking Questions Test

1. Characters outside the picture (for example, the clown's sister)

2. Costume in general (for example, "Why is he wearing those clothes?")

3. Ethnic factors, race, religion, native language, and so on

4. Description of the clown's physical characteristics other than hair

5. Emotions, thinking, personality of clown

6. Family and home of the clown

7. Ground surface

8. Hair

9. Location, setting of figure, and situation

10. Magic

FIGURE 10.1.

11. Occupation and work

12. Pants

13. Physical action related to reflective surface

14. Physical action unrelated to water

15. Reflective surface

16. Shirt

17. Shoes

18. Time, age, past, present, and future

19. Underwater

20. Meaning of the picture as a whole

For example, questions such as, "Where does he come from?" and "Where did he get those pants?" would each receive 1 point. However, if you had asked questions such as, "What color is his hair?" and "What does his hair feel like?" you would receive only 1 point, because both questions fall into category 8. The more different your questions are from each other, the higher your score and your flexibility rating.

A common response to this activity is to ask a question about the clown's hair or shoes and then to ask six or seven more questions about that item. This is in accordance with the directions, but it is not as imaginative as asking seven questions about seven different items in the picture. People who do ask wide-ranging questions are said to be flexible and have also been found to be more imaginative than those who don't.

Now ask your child to take this test. When he is done, go over the scoring with him, explaining the principles of flexibility (using your own words, of course). Try to get him to see how this strategy applies to solving anxiety problems. For example, if he is anxious about speaking in class, ask him to describe every aspect of the problem. Point out to him when he gets overly involved with one aspect of the problem to the exclusion of other relevant factors.

Young children will likely be unable to write down their thoughts or questions, but you can still use the picture to generate questions verbally. This activity is a useful tool for introducing the concept of flexibility in a way that is likely to blossom later.

A New Spin on Grimm

There are numerous children's books available that put a new spin on traditional children's fairy tales and fables. Throughout history, psychologists, researchers, teachers, and caregivers have debated whether fairy tales are too graphic and frightening for young children or whether they actually help children gain mastery over fears and feelings they already possess. Assuming that children are capable of observing and processing stimuli that may promote anxiety, they are also capable of developing skills to counter these perceptions.

Choose a favorite fairy tale, and read or tell the story to your child. Reading the story allows the two of you to focus on illustrations as well as the words and to point to images as you develop alternative actions the characters could take. Take turns pausing in the story to dream up imaginary problems, and make up solutions for them.

As you are speaking with your child, be sure to comment on his attempts to exercise flexible thinking—for example, "Good one! You're really letting your mind open up now!" or "I'm proud of you! You thought up a whole new way Snow White could have done that."

Help your child recognize breakthroughs in his own thinking in real-life situations as well by comments such as, "Did you notice how the problem disappeared as soon as you thought about it in a new way?" or "Maybe we can free up our thinking about this. What are some new ideas?"

A Proverb a Day Keeps Anxiety at Bay

One of the most important factors to remember is communication. Communication between you and your child is as important as communication between you and your partner. You will also want to open lines of communication with others whose expertise you trust. Many problems can be avoided if children feel comfortable speaking about sensitive topics, and caregivers can be informed and take precautions about influences such as peers and the media. This activity is designed to increase communication between you and your children, while at the same time increasing their awareness of perspectives other than their own.

Proverbs are a simple, fun way to encourage children to think laterally, or flexibly, as opposed to vertically and rigidly. Lateral thinking, as discussed by creativity expert Edward deBono (1999), involves looking for alternative ways to define or interpret a problem.

To set up this activity, think of as many proverbs as possible: "The apple doesn't fall far from the tree," "It takes one to know one," "A bird in the hand is worth two in the bush," and so on. Write down the first part of each proverb on a three- by five-inch card. For example, you would write, "The apple doesn't fall . . . ," "It takes one to . . . ," and "A bird in the hand is worth . . ."

Put all the cards in a brown paper bag or a hat. Each player chooses a card and has fifteen seconds to come up with an ending. Although most children will be familiar with the standard ending to these adages, the point of the game is to encourage your child to come up with unique, funny endings. For example, if your child picks, "The apple doesn't fall . . . ," he might come up with the ending, "if you're holding onto it really, really tight." Younger children, who might not be familiar with the proverbs, can play by using nursery rhymes. Read the first line of a rhyme to your child and have him make up the next line, using his own silly rhymes.

You Be Me

This activity is as simple as role playing. Children tend to believe that they are the only person who feels a certain way or, conversely, that everyone feels the way that they do. When they receive images from the media or develop perceptions based on their own experience, they are often unable to filter these images through conversation with others who might interpret the images or sentiments differently. Tell your child that you want to play a game called "You Be Me." He is to pretend that he is the mother (father, aunt), and you will pretend to be him. He should interview you, asking the same kinds of questions that you may have asked him on earlier occasions. Your answers should reflect what you think he is really feeling. After each question, ask him how accurate your answer was.

With an older child, you can simply tell him that you are going to share in your own words how you think he feels about a particular situation that might be contributing to some anxious feelings, for example. Ask your child if your perceptions are accurate. If they are not, you have the opportunity to discuss why they are not.

My Grokking Rock

In his wonderful book *Stranger in a Strange Land* (1961), Robert Heinlein wrote about a magical place called a "grokking rock." This was a rock large enough to sit on, located in a secluded spot where a person could go to think. In the comic strip "Rose Is Rose," the character Rose has a "Let things be" tree that she leans against to relax when she feels stressed. Children are often so scheduled and loaded with activity that they do not have an opportunity to reflect or let go of things that are causing them to feel anxious.

Suggest to your child that he hunt for a favorite rock or other natural resting place near your home. It could be a tree, bush, pond, or something similar. Explain that if his imagination is working properly, he can make that spot into a grokking spot. When he is worrying about something he fears might happen, he can go to his spot and once there will think of a solution to the problem. It will simply come to him there, or he will gain the peace of mind to think more clearly elsewhere. If your child goes there on a regular basis, he could experience a significant reduction in his anxious feelings.

Younger children should be encouraged to find a "thinking place" somewhere inside the house. You can help by building a tent or fort in one room or providing lots of comfortable pillows in a corner of a sunny room.

For many children, but particularly teenagers, the world seems full of contradiction. Teens are encouraged to think for themselves, yet parents and teachers often control much of their lives, such as daily details regarding what work needs to be done, where they are allowed to go, and how they will get there. Teens' bodies are changing rapidly, as are their minds, and they receive messages from peers and the media that may contradict values taught and modeled at home. When some children perceive the world to be contradictory or are unsure how to cope with the messages they receive from various sources, they become anxious. When some children develop a plan to help alleviate these anxious feelings, they often question their ability to follow the plan.

P: PERSISTING IN THE FACE OF OBSTACLES AND FAILURE

Why are some people unwavering in the pursuit of their goals, while other people throw in the towel at the first hurdle? Many factors contribute to the ability to persevere in the face of obstacles, but the main difference between a person who sticks with a plan and one who quits is simple: desire. Anxious children quite often lose their desire to persist with a plan when they are in the midst of dealing with their fears. Their need to protect themselves from frightened feelings overwhelms their zeal for progress, and gradually they lose their drive. It is much easier to make a quick escape than to confront disturbing issues, whether or not the cause of the disturbance is clear or uncertain.

"I Guess It's Not So Scary After All"

When your child feels anxious about a new situation that is approaching, sit down and ask her to think about why she is scared. For a five-year-old, the first day of school might be an example of an ambiguous situation, whereas for a seventeen-year-old, it might be the prom or college tour. Ask your child to give you the number one reason for her anxiety, then numbers two, three, and so on, until she can't think of any more. Write down each reason in order on the left-hand side of a piece of paper. She is likely to say things like, "What if the other kids don't like me?" "What if I don't answer a question right?"

Go through the list, and for each negative, frightening consequence that your child mentions, change it into a positive, exciting one. For example, "What if the other kids don't like me?" can be changed into, "What if I make a lot of good friends?" Write these alternative ideas on the right-hand side of the page on each corresponding line. Read the new list to your child, and ask her to try to see things in a different light: she can feel enthusiasm with the approach of a new situation instead of fear.

Older children may wish to write down their own reasons for feeling anxious. Look at the list and, together with your child, create positive, exciting possibilities out of her negative, frightening ones. Older children can also create artwork, music, or poetry that reflects some feelings they have related to anxiety or creative solutions.

Lessons from a Ring Toss Game

One of the most common concerns of caregivers is that their children don't recognize the risks or consequences associated with their actions. This ties into the notion of invincibility that many teens feel. For example, statements like, "What difference does it make if I have a few drinks? Jeff's driving the car, and he can handle his beer," or "You can't get pregnant the first time," would send most parents running after their children to drag them back into the house. But children don't live or grow in a bubble. One action parents can take is to foster genuine appreciation of risk taking and how children can benefit from taking moderate, responsible risks.

Do you remember playing the game of ring toss? In this game, the farther you are from the pin when you toss the ring, the more points you score for a successful toss. To carry out this activity, you will need to push ten short sticks into the ground at one-foot intervals. The first pin gets a score of 1, the tenth a score of 10. The player gets ten throws. Make a ring from a piece of rope and let your child practice tossing the rope over the sticks. Keep score as she practices.

This game illustrates the concept of risk taking. After she has made thirty or forty tosses, ask your child, "Which pin is the best one to aim at?" She will probably have noticed that she gets the most points by aiming at the middle pin. People who aim at the number one position take a very limited risk, but a ringer is worth only 1 point. Even if they ring the pin ten times, they get a score of only 10. Those who aim at the tenth pin have only one-tenth the likelihood of scoring. Thus, although the tenth pin is worth 10, they're likely to ring it only once, and therefore their maximum possible score is still only 10. If they shoot only at the middle pin, their most likely score would be 25 (five successes times 5 points).

Say to your child, "Although these figures obviously hold only for this game, they probably reflect what happens in the real world. That's the way it is in life too. If you learn to take moderate risks, you're most likely to be successful. Let's talk about what this means when you're trying to deal with scary stuff. What does this ring toss game help you think about?"

Younger children can use buckets and beanbags or a soft non-rubber ball (a rubber ball might bounce out of the buckets) instead of sticks and rings. Because young children have not developed coordination for throwing a ring, throwing a beanbag or ball is easier and serves the same purpose.

Be Like a Seed

In order to gain a sense of mastery over anxiety-provoking situations and to regain some control over their feelings, children benefit greatly from developing skill at delay of gratification. The willingness to endure the stress of prolonged effort so as to reap higher benefit in the long run is the essence of self-control and the underlying theme of this activity.

This activity is designed to help your child gain an appreciation for the greater rewards that can come from controlling the impulse to choose short-term, easier options over more challenging long-term options. In words she can understand, explain to your child the concept of delay of gratification. For example, you might say, "Most of us like to get what we want as soon as possible. It would be nice if that could happen all of the time. However, it seems that most of the best things in life can be had only if we are willing to wait for them and work for them. For instance, if you would like a little plastic toy, you could probably buy it with this week's allowance. But if you want to get a really nice toy, you'll have to save up your allowance for several weeks. It's like that when you are trying to overcome your frightened feelings. It took some time for you to learn to feel afraid; it could take a while for you to learn not to feel afraid any longer. You will have to be patient as you carry out your plan. If you're willing to wait and not give up, you'll surely be successful, and I'll be here to help you."

Show your child how plants grow. Plant a seed (a flower or vegetable—it doesn't matter which) and watch it grow. Suggest to your child that by the time it can be picked, she can have achieved her goal. She can make a deal with herself: "When it blossoms, I blossom!" This is also an opportunity for children to draw or paint the seed as it appears and changes each day or every few days. This becomes a journal of sorts, or record of the seed's progress, and can be referred to in conversation about your child's own progress. Reflecting on her own progress is easier when she has a visual reminder of the slow and steady progress of the seed. These pictures can be referred to again and again in different situations instead of planting a new seed time and time again.

Older children can relate to delay of gratification through experiences relevant to their age group, such as starting to study for a test a week in advance and getting an A versus waiting until the last minute to study and getting a poor grade. She might miss out on a couple of nights watching TV, but the long-term satisfaction of the good grade outweighs the short-term satisfaction of watching TV.

Although delaying gratification may sometimes feel like going on a rough trip, it is ultimately about joy—about the process of working for, waiting for, and finally rejoicing in a greater reward.

Where There's a Will, There's a Way

Anxious children often feel that they have no way out, whether they are explicitly told by someone that they have no choice or because their self-confidence is weak compared to the strength they perceive an older person or authority to possess. When an anxious child becomes rigid in her thinking, she is more likely to be hobbled as she struggles to free herself from her fears. The following activity is designed to promote a sense that when one approach to a problem is not working, there are a number of other techniques that might work.

Children at different ages are drawn to heroes and heroines for different reasons. Choose a book or story where the hero or heroine faces some difficult problem. Read the story aloud with your child, and pause at the end of a description of the heroine's dilemma. At that point, ask your child to suggest a solution to the problem. When she comes up with one, ask her if she can think of another. Continue to ask her to generate alternative solutions until she runs out of ideas. Then read on to find out how the heroine solved the problem. After she does this exercise a couple of times, describe an actual anxiety-producing situation that she faces in her own life, and ask her to try and produce several new ways to deal with it.

Be sure to use appropriate stories with younger children, and ones they can easily understand. You may consider fairy tales to be frightening, so nursery rhymes may be better suited to your child. Children are also very interested in hearing stories about when Mom and Dad were little, so you can create stories from your past to entertain your child and illustrate the point of facing and solving a challenging situation.

Hang On 'Til the Timer Bell Rings

Another activity designed to develop persistence involves thought blocking. Children worrying about the future have a difficult time derailing catastrophic thinking. However, they can learn to control their thoughts well enough to eliminate self-defeating thinking. Caregivers should be mindful of the thoughts children are blocking, in that we need to be receptive to thoughts that children may wish to avoid but may in fact be critical to overcoming some of their fears.

This procedure is best practiced when your child is in the midst of worrying about something. Set a kitchen (or other) timer for a short period of time (about thirty seconds) and ask your child to try to keep from thinking about the troublesome problem. She can try to remember a time when she was really enjoying herself and tell you why the incident was so pleasant. This usually works well because it is impossible to feel happy and agitated at the same time. Soon the thirty seconds will pass, and she has had a successful experience. You can repeat the exercise once or twice (then or later), extending the seconds or minutes on the timer. It is essential that this exercise be practiced until it is mastered so that it may prove successful in the midst of conflict.

If your child is unsuccessful, use a shorter time, but do not give up. Even five seconds is a beginning. When the first five seconds end, your child can try to get another five. It's like the exhausted marathon runner who, near the end of the run, asks herself for just fifty yards, then fifty yards more, until she finally makes it across the finish line. Everyone can block a thought for at least a brief period. Then build on that success. Younger children should begin this exercise with five or ten seconds on the timer.

E: EVALUATING AND ADJUSTING THE PLAN

One way to help your children is to teach them how to evaluate their own progress toward becoming more relaxed and self-confident. There are two kinds of evaluation that are addressed in the activities that follow: formative and summative. Formative evaluation occurs while a plan is in effect, and summative evaluation occurs once a plan has been executed. The two forms of evaluation can be used together to assess how your child is feeling and what changes can be made to the plans designed to reduce his anxious feelings.

Daily Interviews with a Buddy

This activity enlists the support of a good friend or family member. Ask your child to choose a friend whom he sees as being completely trustworthy and to explain to this friend exactly what has been happening with him each day. The buddy might be another family member or perhaps one of your own friends and need not be the same age as your child.

As your child makes this daily report, he will become aware of many details that may well have escaped him in the heat of the day's activities. If the buddy is someone at school or in the neighborhood, your child can make his report in person or over the phone. If the buddy is farther away, your child can use the phone, which may get expensive, or write one letter a day that will be mailed at the end of the week. Older children may find e-mail to be a quick and easy way to communicate with a buddy, and younger children can dictate messages to an adult to transcribe and send via e-mail.

Your child's report should be made in terms of the actions he took and how they worked out, of course, but also should include his feelings. His description of feelings should involve one or the other of two dimensions:

- Qualitative—a subjective evaluation of his feelings ("I felt scared before I started my plan and a little sad about doing this sort of thing, but I felt great when things went okay!")

- Quantitative—how many times or how well he has performed ("I would rate my anxiety level before beginning the plan at about 8. It dropped to about 6 while I was doing it and was down to 3 by the time everything was over.")

As your child speaks to his buddy, he is also hearing himself review how well he has been doing and, through this process, receives invaluable formative evaluation.

Older children can especially benefit from the feedback of a good friend, because friendships are so important at this age. The friend should include both the qualitative and quantitative dimensions in his evaluations. Because anxious children often expect to fail, they might not think they are making progress; an astute friend can point out qualitative and quantitative progress that your child might not have seen on his own.

Rip It to Pieces

When I (L.B.F.) was a student teacher, the children in my classroom had a difficult time getting (and staying) quiet during circle time. One day the head teacher wrote the word "NOISE" in large letters on a two- by three-foot square of butcher paper and hung it on the shelf behind her in the circle. She told the class that at the end of each circle time, the group would assess whether they had been quiet, and if they all agreed that they had, she would let one of the students rip off a piece of the sign. When the sign was all gone, we would have a pizza party. Some days the class did better than others, but this was a strong, visible motivator for them. The children were very invested in this goal and acted as support for each other to remind friends to keep quiet. By the end of the week, there was nothing left of the butcher paper, and from that point on the teacher could simply refer to the big paper to remind children to be quiet.

This concept can be easily translated to your own child's experience with anxious feelings. If your child feels anxious at the start of his day (and many children do as a result of a fresh supply of adrenaline), he could create a sign with an appropriate word on it, such as "SCARED" or "WORRIED." If the fear is related to a particular event, like riding the bus, he can draw corresponding pictures on the sign. The sign needn't be very large, as the main idea is having a tangible representation of feelings that can be made smaller and smaller. At the end of each day, your child can think about how he felt, and if he feels that the anxious feelings weren't present, he can rip a piece off the sign.

This can serve as a checklist in a way too. If he finds it hard to tear off pieces, then perhaps the plan to cope with the anxious feelings should be reevaluated. Thus, the size of the sign at the end of the day can serve not only as a reinforcement for progress made but also as a daily barometer of how well the plan is working.

Three-Times-a-Day Chart

Design a chart for your child like the one shown in Exhibit 10.1. Older children can craft their own charts, but the format should be similar. Decide on three times each day, such as breakfast, lunch, and dinner; morning, midday, and evening; or breakfast, after school, and bedtime when your child will indicate on the chart how he is feeling. Depending on your child's interests or inclinations, he can draw a face to indicate how he is feeling (smiling face = happy; neutral face = mellow, okay; frowning face = sad, angry, frustrated) or a symbol that represents similar feelings (sun = happy; clouds = mellow, okay; rain = sad, angry, frustrated). Craft stores and stationery stores sell a multitude of stickers that represent the same feelings. Children may enjoy choosing stickers, and it is a simple, inexpensive way to engage them in this charting activity.

When your child fills out the chart three times a day, you may be surprised at the results over time. For example, over the course of a week, you may notice that mornings are not happy times for him. His anxiety level may be high. You or your child might have been aware of this without the use of a chart, but it is often difficult to see emotional patterns. Anxious people tend to repress most information about their problems because it is too painful to think about it. This chart is a way to reflect on the patterns indicated in the faces, symbols, or stickers. If mornings are particularly stressful, it might make sense for your child to choose which clothes to wear before going to bed. He can even decide then what to eat for breakfast if that cuts down on time spent making decisions in the morning. Many families find themselves rushed in the morning, so it is a good way for all members to take stock and see how to reduce the chaos at that time of day.

As a result of charting their feelings, many children find that their anxiety has usually lessened by midday, and by dinnertime

EXHIBIT 10.1. Three-Times-a-Day Chart

	Monday	Tuesday	Wednesday	Thursday	Friday	Saturday	Sunday	
Morning								
Midday								
Evening								

they tend to feel much better. This pattern is quite common and is likely due to the generation of adrenaline that occurs as people sleep. Our bodies are hyperalert then because of the large amount of the hormone (adrenaline) surging through our blood. Thus we feel more anxious because we are oriented to feel that way. As the day goes on, we burn up some of our supply just by living, so when we reach dinnertime, we tend to feel calmer. A simple way to reduce extra adrenaline in the morning could be taking a walk around the block or dancing to a favorite song on the radio. There are many physical activities your child could engage in, alone or with a partner, that might make the morning less stressful.

You're a Star!

Cameras can be useful adjuncts to both formative and summative evaluation. There are many uses for snapshots, and with the increasing use of digital cameras and cell phones with this capability, photos can be taken and shared almost instantly, as well as be organized creatively using computer software.

Photography is an especially productive tool when dealing with social phobias like performance anxiety. You can take pictures of your child when he is in the midst of a stressful situation and analyze the photos together. It is important for you to try to take the photos in a relatively unobtrusive way so as to avoid causing additional anxiety. If possible, it is helpful to get some photos of the audience as well.

Show your child the snapshots you have gathered, and ask him to analyze the expressions he sees on his face. Ask him to describe his body language and whether he sees anything in the reaction of his audience. These judgments should help him get a more objective conception of his performance.

Popular magazines are amusing and less threatening ways of examining people's expressions in specific situations. For example, you can use an issue of *Newsweek* or *Time* to find photos of people speaking in public or acting on behalf of others. You can read the text aloud to your child and explain how writers may attempt to analyze the actions of these individuals, much like he is analyzing his own actions. The important point to stress is that no one but the individual knows how he or she is truly feeling at the moment a snapshot is taken. Body language and facial expressions can give us clues, but the true feelings lie inside a person's mind.

It might also be fun to pick up a copy of *The National Enquirer* or *Star*—national magazines that strive to find images of celebrities at their worst. You can compare photos of celebrities in these publications to ones in other magazines, such as *People,* where the celebrities are often well aware that they are being photographed. What does your child notice about the different photos and the different appearance of the people in the photos when they are prepared versus caught off-guard?

This is also an opportunity to speak with your child about how the people in all of these photos are somebody's "star." Your child matters most to you because he is your star, and always will be.

Although home is supposed to be free from fear and worry, it is often while in the confines of a safe, quiet place that our thoughts turn to what is bothering us. All of us want our children to be happy, and it is an unrealistic expectation to believe that children can ever be 100 percent happy. Spending time with your child, focusing on his feelings, and working constructively to support his healthy development is a terrific way to foster a partnership that will continue throughout your lifetimes.

11

HOW CAN YOU COPE WITH YOUR OWN AND YOUR FAMILY'S FEARS?

The serenity to accept the things I cannot change. What an admirable goal! But what a difficult objective. The path to serenity in a threat-filled world is never easy. For one thing, as important a life skill as it is, it's not taught in school and only occasionally touched on in college. Furthermore, different people find serenity in different ways. Nevertheless, much has been discovered in the past two decades by scientists and healers seeking to uncover the nature of self-control. We wish we had many more pages in this book to explore what has been learned. That not being the case, we have endeavored to supply you with a variety of techniques in the hope that you will find several that work well for you. When you do find an approach that helps, try to come up with variations on that theme.

As we have said, your composure under stress is as important as your tactics for keeping your family safe.

COPING WITH YOUR OWN ANXIETIES

Everyone feels anxious when they experience unrelieved stress. At those times, it's wonderful to have someone who can help you cope with that stress, giving you a wise suggestion and a kindly smile. Unfortunately, such a person is not always available. You may have to cope by yourself. The following activities offer you assistance.

Discovering Your Guiding Spirit

Thoughts about your son becoming lost during a hurricane or of your daughter lying injured at home by herself can be devastating. It is hard to persist when you are imagining such horrors, not to mention the everyday troubles that creep into our consciousness. If you would like to gain greater control over your frightening thoughts, you will want to carry out this exercise. It has brought solace and mental control to many.

Choose a room where you can be certain you will not be disturbed. Let's imagine that you are stretching out on a rug or thick towel in the attic. Suffuse the air in the room with the scent of lavender, which encourages deep relaxation. Spray will do, but the method of warming lavender-scented oil over a candle is better. Both are available in health stores. Get into a comfortable position. Then read the following instructions or, better yet, record them, either in your own voice or that of a trusted friend whose voice you like.

Imagine that you are standing in front of a beautiful doorway. The door is crimson, with many rich, intriguing carvings on it. Grasp the door's shiny brass knob, and open it. In front of you, you can see a small landing and a descending staircase. The stairs are covered in a plush brown carpet, and the stairway walls are papered in rich brocade wallpaper, light brown in color. You can see that this is no ordinary stairway. Somehow you understand that it is a beautiful path that will lead you down into the deepest part of your psyche.

Before you descend the stairs, say to yourself that this is a time especially for you. You will think of nothing except the images that I'm asking you to picture. If any other thoughts come to you, you will simply push them away and go on with this enriching experience.

As you walk down the stairs, you find yourself becoming more and more serene. You begin moving down the stairs, starting with the top, the fourteenth stair. Slowly you descend, stepping to the thirteenth stair, the twelfth, the eleventh, the tenth. You are confident that you are where you belong, and this increases your sense of tranquility. You step down to the ninth stair, the eighth, the seventh, the sixth, and though calm, you are also aware that you are entering into a realm of mystery and change. You step down to the fifth stair, the fourth, the third, second, and now you reach the bottom stair.

To your right is a second exquisitely carved door. This one is painted a rich forest green, and it too has an ornate knob. Grasping it, you open the door and see that you are standing on the threshold of a huge, dimly lit room. There is filtered light at the front of the room, and as you step inside and your eyes adjust, you realize that you're in a theater. On your right, you notice banks of chairs steeply angled into the upper reaches of the theater. No one else is here. You are standing between the first-row seats and the stage. In the dim light, you walk along the front edge of the stage until you reach the center chair. You turn and sit, facing the stage.

There's a soft light emanating from under the closed stage curtains. A little tingle of anticipation runs through your body. You know somehow that something really important is about to happen. The curtain slowly opens, and you see a woman standing there. The woman is lit from behind, so you see only her silhouette. You cannot discern who it is, although you can tell from the outline of her clothes that she is female.

Now the footlights along the front edge of the stage begin to brighten, and you can see the person's face. The face may be known to you or may be that of a stranger. It may belong to a woman who is living or deceased, famous or anonymous. Whichever the case, you can see from her beaming smile that she truly understands and loves you. This is an individual who has great power to help you, to give you good advice when you are troubled, to soothe your anxious mind and return you to being a calm, competent problem solver. You feel great joy as you gaze back at this wise sage, this generous guiding spirit. Remain in your seat for a full minute or two, contemplating the deep love that passes between the two of you. Know that this spirit has as much need to help you as you have need of the help.

You would love to continue the wordless communication that has built up between the two of you in these brief moments, but now it is time to leave. The curtain is slowly closing and the footlights are fading. Do not be concerned. When you have need of your guiding spirit, she can be summoned with a thought, to be at your side in an instant. You have only to believe it, and it will happen.

The stage darkens, and reluctantly you stand, turn left, and retrace your steps back to the green door. You open it and begin to climb the stairs, returning to the everyday world and the present.

You can come back to the magic of this theater whenever you desire, but you can also meet with your spirit wherever you are. Come back and sit before the stage when you want the special solace it offers.

Serenely you ascend the stairs: 1, 2, 3, 4, 5, 6, 7, 8, 9, 10, 11, 12, 13, and 14. You're at the top of the stairs before the crimson door, which you open. Now you feel yourself coming back to the place where you started: your rug in the attic. Close the door behind you, and slowly reorient yourself to your surroundings. Wiggle your fingers and your toes, and when you are ready, sit up. Breathing consciously, recall the image of your guiding spirit's face. Remember that from now on, her face can be with you in an instant with a smile of love and wise thoughts that will melt away all your fears. You are safer now than you have ever been before! Be at peace.

Some people find that as they repeat this ritual, changes happen that are beneficial. For example, it may be that a different woman appears to them each time they go down to the theater. Each of these people may have a specialty, an area in which they are especially adept at providing guidance. Some of the spirits that appear may be familiar, and others might be someone surprising or unknown.

On some occasions, it may be that your guiding spirit does have something to say. Open your mind and listen carefully. It may also be that you would like to ask the spirit a question or request specific help.

If you find this activity to be helpful, you may want to share it with your partner, a friend, or your children. You could tape record the instructions for them. For children, you may want to suggest who the spirit is.

Soorya Namaskara—Salute to the Sun

The goal of this activity is to control the muscles, tendons, and ligaments in your body so that on your own, you can reach a state of deep relaxation. Practice this ritual as often as you are able. When you need to become calm, you can summon the feeling of serenity at will. It can be done any place where there is room for you to stretch out to the full length of your body and where you will not be embarrassed to be seen exercising. You will need a clean floor, a pad or rug, and loose clothing.

This exercise is called Soorya Namaskara, which is Sanskrit for "salute to the sun." It is a standard hatha yoga exercise. Its twelve steps are pictured in Figure 11.1.

Take a few deep cleansing breaths. Face the west, the source of calm reflection. Clear your mind of all thoughts, making your mind a blank slate. Take note of Figure 11.1, showing each of the twelve steps in this exercise. Now proceed through the following steps slowly and with deliberate concentration:

1. Stand quietly with your hands pressed together in front of your chest in a prayerful attitude. You are saluting the sun.

FIGURE 11.1. The Twelve Steps of Soorya Namaskara

2. Stretch your arms straight up on either side of your head as high as you can and then bend backward, just to the point where it starts to hurt. Never go past this point on any of the steps.

3. Bend forward and touch the floor with your hands. If you can't reach the floor, just bend your knees until you can.

4. Step one of your feet back so that you are in the runner's starting stance. Give your other leg a good stretch by pressing your

hips toward the floor. Now move your other foot backward until your body forms an upside-down V. Press your heels toward the floor until you can feel the stretch in your calves.

5. Bend your knees, and lower first one knee to the floor, then the other, until both are resting on the floor.

6. Bend your upper body until your chest is also touching the floor. The yogis call this the cat position.

7. Press your hips flat against the floor, and, straightening your arms, stretch your shoulders and head back. If you feel like it, stick your tongue out as far as you can. This is the snake position.

8. Lifting your hips from the floor, put yourself back into the upside-down V position. Push your head forward so that you can see your knees.

9. Stepping one of your feet forward until it is beside the corresponding hand (or as close to this as you can get), give your other leg a good stretch by pressing your hips toward the floor.

10. Move your other foot up so that it is beside your other hand.

11. Slowly resume the standing position, and, spreading your arms, bend backward again.

12. Return to the prayerful stance.

Check your body to see if it is less tense. You will probably notice that you have worked up a light sweat. Although Soorya Namaskara is not an aerobic exercise, it does stretch your muscles, tendons, and ligaments well, and this produces the perspiration. Repeat this same sequence three to five times, then lie down and let yourself relax completely.

You can perform Soorya Namaskara virtually anyplace—you just have to adapt it to the available space. For example, if the only place you can find is a stall in a restroom, you can still perform the bending parts of the ritual (steps 1, 2, 3, 10, 11, and 12).

Think Again!

Among the most likely causes of disruptive anxiety is distortion of the individual's thought process. Cognitive distortions fall into ten categories. As you read the descriptions, you will have a better sense of how such deformed thoughts foster fear and other negative emotions. When you become aware of these thoughts, you can begin to change them (see answers.com/topic/cognitive/distortion).

This activity involves carefully observing your own thinking pattern, searching for any distorted concepts. Such patterns are usually the result of mental errors that happen to be reinforced. Just like superstitions, they quickly become habitual. Then they work as faulty scripts. The simplest way to spot them is by systematically examining the ten categories and creating a chart of examples of as many distorted patterns as you can. After you have generated your inventory, you can start to alter the scripts so they more accurately reflect reality.

It may take time to create this table because you may not have a conscious awareness of your mental errors. Take your time and allow yourself to add to the table as you catch yourself thinking in one of these patterns. Only when you recognize which of your thoughts are distorted are you likely to correct the pattern.

When you feel that you have made a comprehensive list of your typical thoughts, ask a trusted partner to sit with you and have a conversation about the discoveries you made about yourself. Were you aware that there was a name for the kind of thinking that creates your anxiety? Is there one mode of distortion that includes most of your erroneous thoughts? Has your partner observed any other examples of how these distortions are a part of your everyday life? Discuss each example with your partner, and then begin to rewrite these thoughts in a way that more accurately portrays reality.

Your partner can help you work through these thoughts, or you can do this on your own. Either way, it is important to return to your partner when your new list is completed and again discuss your discoveries. Is there a way that you can train your mind to recognize your thought distortions and then change them to be more factual? Is there an area of your life where you can easily improve your reactions? Can you work to completely eliminate one kind of distortion from your vocabulary?

Here is the list of the cognitive distortions and an example of a chart you can use to get started:

Cognitive Distortions

1. *All-or-nothing thinking:* You see things in black and white categories. If your performance falls short of perfect, you see yourself as a total failure.

2. *Overgeneralization:* You see a single negative event as a never-ending pattern of defeat. This is also called *"catastrophizing"*—assuming the worst on the basis of slight evidence.

3. *Mental filter:* You pick out a single negative detail and dwell on it exclusively so that your vision of all reality becomes darkened, like the drop of ink that discolors the entire beaker of water.

4. *Disqualifying the positive:* You reject positive experiences by insisting they "don't count" for some reason or other. You maintain a negative belief that is contradicted by your everyday experiences.

5. *Jumping to conclusions:* You make a negative interpretation even though there are no definite facts that convincingly support your conclusion. There are two types of this distortion:

    Mind reading: You arbitrarily conclude that someone is reacting negatively to you and don't bother to check out the accuracy of your thoughts.

    Fortune teller error: You anticipate that things will turn out badly and feel convinced that your prediction is an already established fact.

6. *Magnification or minimization:* You exaggerate the importance of things (such as your goof-up or someone else's achievement).

Sometimes you do the opposite: you inappropriately shrink things until they appear tiny (your own desirable qualities or the other fellow's imperfections). This is also called the *telescope trick:* your view depends on which end of the telescope you're looking into, but in either case, your vision is distorted.

7. *Emotional reasoning:* You assume that your negative emotions necessarily reflect the way things really are: "I feel angry; someone must have offended me!"

8. *Should statements:* You try to motivate yourself with shoulds and shouldn'ts, as if you have to be whipped and punished before you can obtain your goal. "Musts" and "oughts" are also offenders. The emotional consequence is guilt. When you direct "should" statements toward others, you feel anger, frustration, and resentment.

9. *Labeling and mislabeling:* This is an extreme form of overgeneralization. Instead of describing your error, you attach a negative label to yourself: "I'm a loser." When someone else's behavior rubs you the wrong way, you attach a negative label to him: "What a jerk!" Mislabeling involves describing an event with language that is exaggeratedly colored and emotionally loaded.

10. *Personalization:* You see yourself as the cause of some negative external event for which, in fact, you were not primarily responsible.

As an alternative approach, keep a thought record for a day, noting all the fearful thoughts you have. At the end of the day, use the list of cognitive distortions to go through your thought record and identify the culprits.

Exhibit 11.1 is an example of a chart you might use to categorize your thoughts by distortion. In filling out this chart, you must be courageously honest. After all, what's the point of doing it if you're only going to fool yourself.

EXHIBIT 11.1. My Cognitive Distortions

Cognitive Distortion	Examples of Thoughts	Reality of Situation
1. All-or-nothing thinking		
2. Overgeneralization		
3. Mental filter		
4. Disqualifying the positive		
5. Jumping to conclusions		
6. Magnification or minimization		
7. Emotional reasoning		
8. Should statements		
9. Labeling and mislabeling		
10. Personalization		

Passing On Your Fears

No parents want their children to be anxious. Unfortunately, the best intentions and a loving environment cannot always prevent a child from developing an anxious temperament. Some children are just born worriers.

Parents who have known the challenge of growing up anxious frequently try to prevent that in their child by pushing her into situations she may not be comfortable with. For example, a mother who struggled with extreme shyness as a child may push her child to participate in activities she missed, such as theater or running for school government. Rather than remembering how painful and difficult shyness was for her at her child's age, the mother attempts to mold her child into a confident, aggressive person. But the goal may or may not be appropriate for her child.

Some anxious parents take the opposite stance: rather than force their child to face challenging situations, they overprotect their child by avoiding situations they consider anxiety provoking. By taking this overprotective view, these parents send the message to their child that "this is something scary," and "this is something to worry about." The child with overprotective parents does not learn to experience new challenges at her own pace and learn from her own mistakes.

One of the greatest pitfalls for parents is when, in an attempt to empathize with their child, they decide to share their own anxieties. There is always the temptation to talk with your child in detail about what you know. Unfortunately, children often come to believe that what happened to their parent will inevitably happen to them too. For example, we adults know that germs can make us sick, so it is important to wash our hands after using the bathroom or touching something dirty. However, children may become excessively anxious about cleanliness and germs if they are given a detailed account of how you once caught the flu from a toilet seat and had to receive antibiotics shots.

Whether parents force their child to face all challenges or protect their child from all new trials, the result is that the child learns to be afraid and insecure in her own ability to cope with her anxieties. Parents need to ask themselves whether they are trying to help their anxious child or compensate for anxieties of their own. The best course is to learn to recognize your child's own strengths and weaknesses, as well as your own strengths and weaknesses, and to work with the assets, regardless of your own personal experiences with anxiety.

The Power of Prayer

Spirituality serves a variety of roles in an individual's life. For instance, it can be a source of comfort for an individual in a time of stress. There is research that suggests that people who believe in the possibility of assistance from a higher power are more resilient and display less anxiety when they are faced with adversity. Therefore, it is important to engage your family in some type of weekly spiritual activity. Here is a method you might use.

Many Catholics obtain strength and serenity from saying the rosary. This involves repeating certain prayers such as the "Hail, Mary" in a set sequence. The repetition itself is soothing and may have positive effects on the subconscious mind, as well as being spiritually advantageous. If you and your family are not practicing Catholics, you may know other prayers that are soothing in a similar way. You may also design your own brief prayers that you recite while holding an object that embodies spirituality as you define it. Your prayers would probably address the twin goals of help with your plans for safety and for peace of mind for each of you. All family members could have a set of beads or another spiritual object. On a regular basis (once a day, once a week), you would get together and say the prayers. Soon you will have memorized them, and the act of saying them will induce a sense of tranquility. You could kneel as you say them or just sit around a table.

It is important that you have beads or some other kind of amulet—perhaps knotted strings, colored chips, or sticks with special markings on them. Alternatively, you might want to light a candle with each prayer or turn on a little colored Christmas tree light bulb. You will find that after a while, whatever object you use takes on a power of its own, a power that your prayers have infused into it. Then just holding the object itself, in addition to your prayers, will contribute to your sense of control and relaxation.

Parenting Styles

One of the most important influences on your child's personality is your parenting style. Scientists have identified five distinct styles: authoritarian, permissive, authoritative, democratic, and nurturing parenting. Try to read about each of them with an open mind, trying to realize which style you and your partner, if you have one, most often follow. We believe that one of them is most likely to foster courage and self-confidence in your children.

Authoritarian Parenting. Parents who use the authoritarian style are highly demanding and unresponsive to their children's wishes. It is the "my-way-or-the-highway" mentality that emphasizes conformity and obedience. At the same time, such parents are disinterested in the child's point of view. If parents and child were each granted a vote (in a two-parent household) when making decisions, parents would have two votes and the child would have none. Children are expected to accept their parents' decisions without question, and punishment usually follows disobedience. Children of authoritarian parents tend to be the most anxious and distant. A child who is not allowed to make independent decisions does not have the opportunity to experience the consequences of success and failure, and so has little practice in making good judgments.

Permissive Parenting. On the opposite end of the spectrum, the permissive parenting style makes very low demands on children.

Furthermore, it is extremely accepting because parents either approve of their child's desires (philosophical permissiveness) or really don't care much (disengaged permissiveness). In this type of household, the child gets three votes, and the parents have none. In the first subcategory, parents choose to be permissive because of their philosophical stance regarding parenting. This hands-off philosophy allows children to make virtually all of their own decisions, even when they may not be qualified to do so. It is a high-risk parenting style, because sometimes children make very poor decisions.

These parents do not enforce curfews or stress learning manners. They have a strong belief that when children are given freedom, they will almost always make decisions that are good for them. They will get lots of practice in decision making. This philosophy was espoused by the French philosopher Jean-Jacques Rousseau and by the British educator A. S. Neill in his book *Summerhill* (1993), which was popular in the 1960s, when it was first published.

The other type of permissive parenting results not from a personal philosophy or belief system but because the parents are simply disengaged. At its extreme, this type of parenting may be considered neglect, for the parents exhibit minimal commitment to their children and their role as parents. They usually display little warmth, emotional and physical, to their child, and may even suffer from depression. Aside from providing the bare minimum in terms of feeding and clothing their child, disengaged parents show little interest in their child's well-being. They may be struggling with stresses in their own lives, such as divorce, substance abuse, or lack of income, which makes it difficult for them to find the energy and motivation to focus on the needs of their child.

Unfortunately, disengaged parenting has a negative impact on the child's development. Children in such families fail to form some of the basic building blocks for successful later development, such as attachment, social and emotional skills such as sharing and empathy, and self-esteem. If the child perceives that she is not valued as a part of her family, she may come to expect that she is not worthy of love and respect from others. It may seem contradictory, but children who grow up in permissive households tend to crave rules and guidelines, since they provide the security and consistency that their homes lack.

Authoritative Parenting. Authoritative child rearing leans toward the authoritarian style of parenting. In authoritative households, reasonable demands are placed on children, and parents enforce limits and discipline with rational explanations tempered with love. Parents express love and acceptance openly and encourage the child's participation when family decisions are made. Parents in an authoritative household get two votes to the child's one vote, because the parents possess wisdom and experience that the child does not. Parents are responsible for the health and well-being of their child and reserve the right to exercise their majority vote if they feel that their decision is in the best interest of their child. The important element of this parenting style is respect: parents respect the rights of their child and the child respects the parents' input.

Democratic Parenting. The democratic parenting style refers to the honest communication between parents and their child. For example, democratic decisions are reached by mutual agreement, where the parents receive a total of one vote and the child receives one vote. Parents and child are on equal footing in the decision-making process, and the child's input is actively sought and respected by the parents.

When parents choose to enforce discipline, they provide reasons for doing so. In this respect, democratic parenting is similar to authoritative parenting. The difference lies in the fact that parents and child are equals in the democratic household. Children who are used to getting their own way find it difficult to obey someone else's demands. Although these children may tend to be more rebellious than children raised in nondemocratic homes, they also tend to be highly curious and creative.

Nurturing Parenting. A fifth parenting style that encourages a child's creativity, sense of responsibility, and social skills has been identified by John Dacey and Alex Packer in their book, *The Nurturing Parent*. This type of parent tries to foster their child's development every day in as many ways as possible. Nurturing parents instill confidence and persistence in their children, which results in their abilities to seek out creative outlets and achieve imaginative outcomes.

In terms of the hypothetical votes parents and child hold in nurturing households, the number is zero. Neither parents nor child has a vote in the decision-making process. Rather, the decisions tend to be reached through a continuous give-and-take evaluative process. For example, parents trust their child's judgment because they trust that they have demonstrated fairness as role models.

As a result of this trust, nurturing parents have fewer rules for their children to follow. This was a significant finding for Dacey and Packer when they interviewed the teenaged participants of their study, for they observed that the absence of rules did not mean absence of discipline, as is the case with permissive parenting. Nurturing parents do set limits, but indirectly rather than explicitly. Nurturing parents do protect their children from hurting themselves or others not by making demands but by communicating values and discussing their child's behavior. If at all possible, they go along with their children's decisions, even allowing actions they know will probably not succeed. They do this because of their faith that experience is the best teacher and because lots of practice in making judgments makes for better judging.

Not all parents feel comfortable with such an open and apparently unstructured system. Remember that what is most effective in one home may not be effective in another household or with one set of parents as opposed to another. Ultimately you are the experts who can determine the most comfortable fit for your own family. No matter how you spend time with them, if it is caring and attentive, your children will be safer.

HELPING YOUR WHOLE FAMILY COPE WITH ANXIETY

A vital component of maintaining your equilibrium is your ability to help the other members of your family maintain theirs. In the sections that follow, we suggest ways that assist you in achieving this equally important goal.

How to Get Your Children to Tell You Their True Feelings About School (and Anything Else)

Many times children develop school phobia or a strong dislike of school for reasons they don't want to tell you. This reticence is problematic for them, because it means they have to worry about your finding out their true feelings, and for you, because consciously or unconsciously, you will probably know they are withholding something, and this will cause you concern.

They may say school is boring or they don't like their teachers, when in fact, they're scared of other kids. Often they haven't even been bullied themselves, but they've seen it happen to others, and they feel threatened that their turn is next. Why don't they admit to these fears? They may be ashamed that they don't stand up to the bully, or guilty that they want bullying to happen to someone else. Or there may be other reasons that they don't want to reveal.

So how to get to the heart of the problem? Psychologists have developed a technique called *reflective listening*. This method has five principles; if you observe them carefully, you are quite likely to get your children to open up to you:

- *Watch your child's face and body language.* Your child may assure you that he or she does not feel sad, but a quivering chin or too-bright eyes will tell you otherwise. A child may deny feeling frightened, but if you put your fingers on her or his wrist as a caring gesture, you may discern a pounding heart. When words and body language don't align, the child's body language is usually closer to the truth.

- *Rephrasing*. Reword your child's statements in ways that might be less self-critical. For example, if your child says, "Jimmy is a total wimp; he didn't dare to stick up for me!" you can say, "You feel your brother isn't always as brave as he could be?" This is better wording, because when anyone harbors negative feelings about a family member, he or she also is likely to feel negatively about being a family member. If a teenager shouts, "Dad is nothing but a lousy souse," you can say, "I guess you think your father drinks too much sometimes." No one wants to be thought of as a drunkard's child. In a subtle way, your words say, "I don't see you as the son of a drunk." These subtle rephrasings make your child more able to discuss things with you.

- *Give nonverbal support*. This may include a smile, a hug, a wink, a pat on the shoulder, nodding your head, making eye contact, or holding your child's hand or wrist.

- *Use the right tone of voice for what you are saying*. Remember that your voice tone communicates as clearly as your words. Make sure your tone does not come across as sarcastic or all-knowing. Softer, lower tones are usually calming and imply that you care.

- *Use encouraging phrases to show your interest and to get your child talking*. Helpful little phrases, spoken appropriately during pauses in the conversation, can communicate how much you care:

"Oh, really?"

"Anyone would have been frightened by that!"

"That must have made you feel sad."

"Tell me more about that."

"Then what happened?"

If you are judgmental or critical, your child may decide that you just don't understand. Reflective listening is a better solution. You cannot be a good influence on a child who won't talk to you.

Encouraging Courage

Given the ready availability of drugs and alcohol in our society, it takes a lot of self-control and, yes, courage, to withstand the ever-present temptations. Extolling the virtue of courage, and modeling it whenever possible, can make a solid contribution to cultivating this invaluable trait in your children.

In his recent book, *Raising Courageous Kids* (2004), Charles Smith suggests five actions that he has found promote courageous attitudes in children:

- Be a model of what you consider important. This means setting good examples and maintaining reasonable limits.

- Provide "power moments." Create challenges that are moderately difficult, and then provide support so that your child is likely to be successful.

- Protect without smothering. Identify reasonable risks, and try to protect your children unobtrusively, so they can experience the joy of accomplishment without feeling you hovering over them. When I (J.S.D.) was a young father, my five-year-old daughter wanted to walk to the other end of the street. After much discussion of safety rules, we let her, but I followed, ducking from tree to tree so she wouldn't think we didn't trust her. When I got back, my wife was laughing. "If anyone had seen what you were doing," she giggled, "they would have called the police on a stalker!"

- Acknowledge your children's fears. Show them that fear is okay and needn't be accompanied by shame.

- Make an investment of time. As Smith says, "Do things with them, not just for them."

Amulets

An amulet is any object that is worn or carried in the hope that in some way, it will help to improve a person's life. The concept has a long history. Ancient Egyptians wore amulets on necklaces, and the Greeks carried protective charms called *phylakterion* with them wherever they went. These objects were usually a stone or a piece of metal with an inscription or some figures engraved on it.

Early Christians often wore the tiny symbol of a fish, for which the Greek word is *ichthys*. This word also contains the initials of the Greek words for "Jesus Christ, Son of God, and Savior." Letters of the archaic runic alphabet, used by the early Scandinavians, may still be seen on amulets. They carved individual letters into wood and stone and carried them for symbolic protection.

Today the homes of many observant Jews have a mezuzah—a slip of parchment on which passages from the Torah are written and placed in a tiny case that is attached to the doorways of their homes. These are seen as protection from evil spirits and other harms. Small versions of the mezuzah can be worn on a chain as a necklace. Catholics sometimes wear necklaces called "scapulars," and they and other Christians may wear a small crucifix.

We have numerous synonyms for the word *amulet: talisman, charm, trinket, totem, sacred tool,* and *magical object,* but they all mean an object that has been blessed or otherwise empowered to achieve some task. It has been a common practice throughout history to create amulets by placing them on an altar and smudging them with some kind of special smoke—a burning bundle of dried sage leaves, for example. They are also created by being blessed by some person believed to have special powers. A set of rosary beads blessed by the pope is an example.

Amulets may also be empowered through group ceremonies. An example is the AA medallion. Members of Alcoholics Anonymous receive a special medal each year on the anniversary of the date they stopped drinking. The presentation is made during a ceremony, and the medallion itself is embossed with St. Francis's prayer and other meaningful symbols. Recovering alcoholics carry it with them as an aid to not take a drink. Another instance is a wedding bouquet. Because it has been carried by the bride, many believe that it takes on the power to help an unmarried woman find a suitable mate in the near future.

Humans are the only animals that know how to empower objects, which then can have power over them. It's a magical ability. You may want to create your own powerful amulet to help you when you feel afraid. You might also want to craft amulets for your children. This next story explains one way of doing it, but you should consider inventing your own techniques.

THE MAGIC MEDALLION (J.S.D.)

When my granddaughter was five, her mother told me that she was becoming upset by thunderstorms and asked me to suggest a remedy. I selected an object that might serve as an amulet to ward off her fearful feelings. I chose a brass medallion that had been given to me decades ago. My granddaughter knew that it was important to me, and even though the inscription and diagram on it meant nothing to her, the medallion had the look of something special.

The next step was to consecrate it on the little altar I have built in a shed on the back of my property. The altar consists of a wooden tray affixed across a window, which contains raked sand and a few special objects that I use for meditation. We placed the medallion on the sand in the middle of the altar. Then we lit a bundle, called a smudge, of white sage. My granddaughter waved the small smoking bundle back and forth over the medallion while I read the following words aloud:

"We are here today because we want to help this child. We want to help her not to be afraid of the noisy old thunder. The way we are going to help her is by putting magic into the special medal that is on this altar. First we're going to bless it.

We want to put our strongest wishes into it so that it can protect her from being frightened. When there's a thunderstorm, we want her to pick up this medal and hold it tightly in her hand. She should realize that her whole family wants her to know that she is safe and does not have to be afraid. It will be just as though we are all there with her, putting our arms around her, and protecting her from her fears. When she uses this medal, she can be certain that she will be okay."

We then took the medal to other members of the family and asked them to hold it while they said a prayer to give her courage. It worked. During the next several storms, she used the medal, and today she no longer needs it.

Brainstorming

First developed by Alex Osborn, an executive of a major advertising firm, brainstorming is a technique designed to help small groups produce high-quality ideas. He argues that producing ideas should be distinct from the evaluation of their worth. Osborn had observed that because most problem-solving conferences are based on the principles of debate, they seldom hatch creative solutions. In most such meetings, criticism of the participants' thoughts plays a large role. Brainstorming sessions are guided by a different set of rules:

- There must be no criticism of ideas. Often a facilitator is chosen whose job it is to ring a bell if any criticism occurs.
- Participants strive to avoid editing their own ideas, consciously or unconsciously.
- Wild, funny, or even silly ideas are welcome. Even if they seem to be ridiculous, they frequently spawn high-quality thoughts in others.
- Production of a large quantity of suggestions is encouraged.

- Building on the contributions of others is welcome.

- Suggestions are tape-recorded or jotted down by a group secretary.

- Only when the group feels it has exhausted all the possibilities are the suggestions evaluated.

Here's an example of how brainstorming works. In the late 1940s, a group was charged with figuring out how to dispose of the glass from junked automobiles. The metal and rubber from the cars could be recycled, but the reinforced glass could not be reused. The group produced many ideas for getting rid of the broken shards: dump them in the ocean, throw them down a mine shaft, and many others, all of them expensive.

One man in the group became bored with the conversation and began thinking about taking his son to the carnival that night. He imagined all the things they would do, and for some reason, his mind fastened onto the cotton candy machine. He couldn't stop picturing the molten candy being sprayed out against a spinning cylinder. Just fooling around, he said, "I know. Let's melt the stuff and spray it around on a board, see if we get any pretty patterns."

Some people chuckled at his lighthearted irrelevance, but someone else said, "Wait a minute. You might have something there! Maybe if we sprayed molten glass against a rotating cylinder, we could make sheets of the stuff, any thickness we want. It would probably be tough and yet pliable. Let's give that a try!"

Maybe the actual process wasn't quite that simple, but eventually that group at Corning Glass invented fiber glass, which has proven so amazingly useful in making boats, appliances, and automobile bodies. In no time, there were no more smashed-up car windows to be had. They had changed a costly expense, discarding junk, into a valuable asset.

Many studies have demonstrated that these brainstorming rules work. If you and your family can succeed in applying them to your plans, you will achieve a higher-quality result.

❧

Dealing with anxiety effectively, regardless of whether your solutions are rational: that is what we sincerely hope this book will help you do. Remember that moderation and balance are the keys, and not underprotection or overprotection.

If you think one of us can help you further, e-mail us at lfiore@lesley.edu or dacey@bc.edu. We can respond only to very specific questions by e-mail, however; it would be unprofessional to do otherwise. Nevertheless, give us a try if you wish. We wrote this book because we both feel great sympathy and empathy for the stresses the modern world causes so many parents. We truly wish you well!

LISTS OF INTERNET SITES, BY TYPE OF THREAT

This appendix lists helpful Internet sites arranged by chapters in this book. Most of them are about steps you can take to make your family safer. However, we remind you that spending inordinate amounts of time searching the Web for safety ideas runs counter to our main premise: moderation, moderation, moderation. Take a quick tour of the sites that look promising to you. Selecting a few that you find most useful is probably a good idea. Also, if you believe that a chapter in this book covers its topic inadequately, here's your chance to remedy the fault.

WEATHER SAFETY

http://www.weather.com/safeside
http://www.nhc.noaa.gov/HAW2/english/disaster_prevention.shtml
http://www.wmo.int/disasters/
http://www.newton.dep.anl.gov/askasci/wea00/wea00049.htm
http://www.srh.noaa.gov/oun/severewx/safety
http://www.weather.gov/om/winter/index.shtml
http://www.strikingimages.com/safety.htm
http://www.weatherwizkids.com/WxSafety.htm

KIDNAPPING

www.fbi.gov/mostwant/kidnap/kidmiss.htm

www.vca.org

www.getbestinfo.com

www.missingkids.com/missingkids/servlet/ResourceServlet?
LanguageCountry=en_US&PageId=895–19k

www.womenslaw.org/custody.htm60k

www.naswdc.org/resources/abstracts/abstracts/ParentalKidnapping.
asp-43k

www.answers.com/topic/elizabeth-smart-kidnapping-51k

https://www.thesafeside.com/store/default.asp?CartSourceID=11

http://danger.mongabay.com/kidnapping.htm

TERRORISM

http://www.dhs.gov/dhspublic/theme_home6.jsp

http://www.epa.gov/

http://www.epa.gov/epahome/children.htm

http://www.guttmacher.org/pubs/tgr/04/6/gr040613.pdf

http://www.firstgov.gov/Topics/Usgresponse/Protect_Yourself.shtml

http://lacoa.org/esp-page/Focus/Focus_04/04–05%20Biological%
20Threats.pdf

http://www.nj.com/business/expresstimes/index.ssf?/base/
business-1/1105265117175910.xml

http://www.vdes.state.va.us/prepare/terrorismtoolkit/terrguide/
intro/response

http://www.healthinschools.org/sh/bioresource.asp

http://www.milwaukee.gov/display/displayFile.asp?docid=
398&filename=/User/mbrues/FAQ-BioThreats.htm

http://www.protectionagainstcrime.com/text/bomb-threats.html

http://www.hpac.com/microsites/hsb/blewett_hsbsup/blewett_
hsbsup.htm

MEDIA

http://www.aap.org/family/mediaimpact.htm
http://www.WiredSafety.org/
http://www.safekids.com/kidsrules.htm
http://www.safekids.com
http://www.ccmostwanted.com/kids/iguide.htm
http://web6.duc.auburn.edu/outreach/ask_alabama/december2004/
    Logo%20Report%20on%20Children%20&%20Internet%
    20December%202004.pdf
http://www.gannett.com/go/difference/greatfalls/pages/part6/
    traced.html
http://www.childdevelopmentinfo.com/health_safety/video_
    game_rating_system.htm
http://www.pcworld.com/howto/article/0,aid,122116,00.asp

DRUG AND ALCOHOL ABUSE

www.state.ma.us/dph/inhalant
www.hometownsource.com
www.drugfree.com
http://www.whitehousedrugpolicy.gov/publications/factsht/
    juvenile/index.html
http://www.christophers.org/NN_404.html
http://www.fsis.usda.gov/FOIA/dir/47354Rev2.pdf
http://www.state.gov/documents/organization/10492.pdf
http://newsfromrussia.com/science/2005/01/11/57799.html

CHILD ABUSE

http://www.missingkids.com/en_US/documents/nismart2_
familyabduction.pdf

http://www.law.indiana.edu/pop/domestic_violence/

http://www.police.nashville.org/bureaus/investigative/domestic/
symptoms.htm

http://www.gov.pe.ca/infopei/index.php3?number=56751&
lang=E

http://www.religioustolerance.org/hom_stud.htm

http://www.channel4.com/health/microsites/F/family/problems/
abuse.html

http://www.opdv.state.ny.us/about_dv/fss/trapped.html

http://www.drirene.com/physical.htm

http://www.safecanada.ca/link_e.asp?category=13&topic=110

SCHOOL VIOLENCE

www.myscschools.com/tracks/educators/safeschl/-26k

www.rppi.org/ps234.html-398k

www.keepschoolssafe.org/-12k

www.hayessoft.com

www.mentalhealth.samhsa.gov/schoolviolence/links.asp-25k

www.nap.edu

www.teachsafeschools.org

www.ThePeaceCompany.com

www.questia.com

www.rand.org/publications/IP/IP219/-36k

www.familyeducation.com/article/0,1120,1–6471,00.html-36k

http://www.ccboe.net/psychology/safety.html

http://www.micheleborba.com/Pages/ArtBMI01.htm

www.i-safe.org

www.mindoh.com

www.cyberbully.org

HOME SAFETY

http://www.homesafetycouncil.org/index.aspx
http://www.safewithin.com/index.cgi
http://www.safewithin.com/homesafe
http://www.nsc.org/
http://www.nsc.org/library/facts.htm
www.thesafetyexpert.com
http://www.epa.gov/epahome/citizen.htm
http://kidshealth.org/parent/firstaid_safe/home/household_
    checklist.html
http://www.mctf.org/sp.aspx?id=203
http://www.ExpertClick.com/NewsReleaseWire/default.cfm?
    Action=ReleaseDetail&ID=8558

GENERAL THREATS

www.aap.org
http://www.ocfs.state.ny.us/main
http://www.cwla.org/programs/childprotection/
    childprotectionfaq.htm
http://www.4children.org/news/901haz.htm
http://directory.google.com/Top/Society/People/Women/Issues/
    Violence_and_Abuse/Domestic_Violence/Legal_Issues/
http://familymanagement.com/facts/english/
http://www.actionchildprotection.org/books.htm
http://www.childrensaidsociety.org/media/file/
    protctnfrmdomesticabuseinfct.pdf
http://www.womenshealth-naturalsolutions.com/index.html
http://www.ocipep.gc.ca/info_pro/checklists/index_e.asp
http://www.solgen.gov.ab.ca/tips/families.aspx
http://www.apahelpcenter.org/articles/
http://www.homesafetycouncil.org/
http://www.safewithin.com/index.cgi

http://www.nsc.org/
http://www.nsc.org/library/facts.htm
http://ezinearticles.com
http://www.calpoison.org/public/top_10_prevent.pdf
http://www.mctf.org/sp.aspx?id=203
http://www.eslteachersboard.com/cgibin/traveling/
    index.pl?noframes;read=1429w.gentleparents.com/albright.html
http://www.wickedgoodhomes.com/articles/501_
    childsafehomes.htm
http://www.emediawire.com/releases/2004/12/prweb191080.htm
http://www.expertclick.com
http://www.liliguana.com

REFERENCES AND FURTHER READING

American Psychological Association. *School Bullying Is Nothing New.* 2006a. http://www.psychologymatters.org/bullying.html.

American Psychological Association. *Violent Video Games.* 2006b. http://www.psychologymatters.org/videogames.html.

Anderegg, D. *Worried All the Time: Rediscovering the Joy in Parenthood in an Age of Anxiety.* New York: Free Press, 2003.

Dacey, J. "A History of the Concept of Creativity." In H. H. Gardner and R. Sternberg (eds.), *Encyclopedia of Creativity.* Orlando, Fla.: Academic Press, 1999.

Dacey, J., and Fiore, L. *Your Anxious Child.* San Francisco: Jossey-Bass, 2000.

Dacey, J., Kenny, M., and Margolis, D. *Adolescent Psychology.* (4th ed.) Houston: Thomson, 2005.

Dacey, J., and Lennon, K. *Understanding Creativity: The Interplay of Biological, Psychological and Social Factors.* San Francisco: Jossey-Bass, 1999.

Dacey, J., and Packer, A. *The Nurturing Parent.* New York: Simon and Schuster, 1992.

Dacey, J., and Travers, J. *Human Development Across the Lifespan.* (6th ed.) New York: McGraw-Hill, 2006.

Dacey, J., and Weygint, L. *The Joyful Family.* San Francisco: Conari Press, 2002.

deBono, E. *Six Thinking Hats.* Boston: Back Bay Press, 1999.

Elkind, D. *The Hurried Child: Growing Up Too Fast and Too Soon.* (3rd ed.) New York: Perseus, 2001.

Heinlein, R. *Stranger in a Strange Land.* New York: Putnam, 1961.

Koster, R. *A Theory of Fun for Game Designers*. Scottsdale, Ariz.: Para-glyph Press, 2005.

Neill, A. *Summerhill*. New York: St. Martin's Press, 1960; rev. 1993.

Ochs, E., and Taylor, C. "Storytelling as a Theory-Building Activity." *Discourse Processes*, 1992, 15(1), 37–72.

"Preparing for Disasters." *Harvard Public Health Review*, Winter 2006, pp. 8–11.

Robertson, J. *Apocalypse Chow*. New York: Simon Spotlight Entertainment, 2005.

Smith, C. *Raising Courageous Kids: Eight Steps to Practical Heroism*. Notre Dame, Ind.: Sorin, 2004.

Tarbox, K. *A Girl's Life Online*. New York: Penguin, 2004.

Tippin, K. "Out of Bounds: Sexual Abuse by Coaches: Violation of Athletes, Their Trust." Summer 2003. http://www.mediarelations.k-state.edu/WEB/News/Webzine/0202/sexualabuse.html.

Warner, J. *Perfect Madness: Motherhood in the Age of Anxiety*. New York: Penguin, 2006.

ABOUT THE AUTHORS

John S. Dacey has taught developmental psychology at Boston College for forty years and has been a licensed psychotherapist since 1973. With Lisa Fiore, he is the author of a book on a related subject, *Your Anxious Child,* and has published eleven other books and thirty articles in scholarly journals in the field of development. He has appeared on NBC's *Today* program and National Public Radio and has been interviewed nearly fifty times for top-level radio programs, magazines, and newspapers. He is the father of three daughters and grandfather of nine grandchildren and lives with his wife in Lexington, Massachusetts.

Dacey himself is a survivor of a serious anxiety disorder resulting from a fire that took the lives of his mother, two sisters, and two brothers; he knows how devastating fear can be. As a result of his work in this field, his anxiety problems have almost completely abated.

Lisa B. Fiore teaches early childhood education and elementary education courses at Lesley University in Cambridge, Massachusetts. She is a licensed early childhood teacher for grades K–3. Fiore has appeared on FOX News and NBC News broadcasts commenting on topics relating to child development and has been interviewed in multiple publications, including *Parents, Parenting,* and *Family Digest.*

Fiore's academic background in early childhood has taken on a whole new meaning since the births of her two children, now ages four and two, and she can well relate to the challenges parents face as they strive to raise confident and secure young children. She and her husband practice their parenting skills and laugh often at their home in Belmont, Massachusetts.

INDEX

E

Earthquakes: during, 24; after, 25; preparation for, 23–24
Educational abuse, 105
Egyptians, ancient, 183
Electricity, wide scale loss of, 57–58
Elkind, D., 6–7
Emergency Action Questionnaire, 54, 57–59
Emory University, 77–78
Emotional abuse, 95. *See also* Child abuse
Emotional reasoning, 172, 173
Encouraging phrases, 181
Entertainment Software Ratings Board Web site, 69
Eye of the storm, 29

F

Failure, persisting in face of, 15
Family: cohesion, 12–13; shrinking size of, 7
Family Circle magazine, 70
Family, extended, 7–8
Fears: passing on, 174–175; scaling, 142–143
Federal Emergency Management Agency (FEMA), 27, 33, 34, 39
Feelings, child's true, 180–182
FEMA. *See* Federal Emergency Management Agency
Fiber glass, 186
Fight-or-flight response, 13, 14
Fiore, L., 3, 13
Flight Simulator (video game), 67

Floods, 57–58; during, 27; after, 27–28; preparation for, 26–27; statistics about, 24–25
Fortune teller error, 171
friendster.com (Web site), 67

G

GFSA. *See* Gun-Free Schools Act
Girl's Life Online, A (Tarbox), 67
Global terrorism, 3
Goldfarb, B., 19–21
Goldfarb, R., 19–21
Good News/Bad News Scale, 4 *Fig.* 1.1
Google toolbar, 64
Gorelli, R., 111–112
Grand Theft Auto (video game), 68
Gratification, delay of, 153–154
Greeks, ancient, 183
Grokking rock, 150
Guiding spirit, discovering, 164–167
Gun-Free Schools Act (GFSA), 114

H

Harvard University, 30
Heart rate, knowing, 140–141
Heinlein, R., 150
Helicopter moms, 121
Helplessness, learned, 7
Home invasion, 57–58
Home safety, 5; Internet sites on, 193
Honeywell Corporation, 42–43
Humor, 141–142

X

Y

Z